MAKER LITERACY

MAKER LITERACY

A New Approach to Literacy Programming for Libraries

LYNN PAWLOSKI AND CINDY WALL

 **LIBRARIES UNLIMITED**™

An Imprint of ABC-CLIO, LLC

Santa Barbara, California • Denver, Colorado

Library of Congress Cataloging-in-Publication Data

Names: Pawloski, Lynn M., author. | Wall, Cindy R., author.
Title: Maker literacy : a new approach to literacy programming for libraries / Lynn Pawloski and Cindy Wall.
Description: Santa Barbara, CA : Libraries Unlimited, [2017] | Includes bibliographical references and index.
Identifiers: LCCN 2016029841 (print) | LCCN 2016045603 (ebook) | ISBN 9781440843808 (paperback : acid-free paper) | ISBN 9781440843815 (ebook)
Subjects: LCSH: Children's libraries—Activity programs. | Makerspaces in libraries. | Maker movement in education. | Technological literacy—Study and teaching—Activity programs. | Children's software—Reviews. | Mobile apps—Reviews. | Children's libraries—Activity programs—United States—Case studies.
Classification: LCC Z718.3 P39 2017 (print) | LCC Z718.3 (ebook) | DDC 027.62/5—dc23
LC record available at https://lccn.loc.gov/2016029841

ISBN: 978-1-4408-4380-8
EISBN: 978-1-4408-4381-5

21 20 19 18 17   3 4 5

This book is also available as an eBook.

Libraries Unlimited
An Imprint of ABC-CLIO, LLC

ABC-CLIO, LLC
130 Cremona Drive, P.O. Box 1911
Santa Barbara, California 93116-1911
www.abc-clio.com

This book is printed on acid-free paper ∞

Manufactured in the United States of America

"I hear and I forget. I see and I remember.
I do and I understand."—*Confucius*
—LP

To Anne, the best friend ever, who always believed.
—CW

CONTENTS

INTRODUCTION

The Maker Movement might initially be perceived as the creation of concrete things: objects that can be picked up and held in one's hands, manipulated, played, worked, used for decoration or given as gifts, and so on. But the Maker Movement also applies to ideas, feelings, and thoughts: conceptual *things* that can also be formed, transmuted, used, and shared.

One benefit of the Maker Movement is its ability to connect people who share similar passions and interests: people who crochet pass along tips, patterns, and handmade goods; farmers and would-be farmers post chicken-coop designs and modifications; and writers share themes, reflections, revisions, and inspiration. The role of librarians has always been about connecting people with ideas and ideas with people. This rooted, traditional concept now stands on the precipice of change. At a time when society is lamenting the loss of personal interactivity, libraries are becoming the centers of makers, sharers, and communities.

The library can be a place where children associate fun with learning, making, sharing, and building. At library programming, children should have the opportunity to learn age-appropriate literacy skills, develop awareness of different points of view that shape ideas and processes, and discover cross-curricular connections between different disciplines. Actively "Making" things helps children process and retain the information you wish to impart at your library programs. Examples of things created from programs in this book include films, sculptures, computer code, and more.

Offering Maker Literacy programming furthers the library's role as a community center where people share ideas, supplies, methods, time, books, technology, and/or the tools they might not have at home. In addition, they pass their knowledge along to other people with similar interests, both at the library and at large. In this way, users build a community at the library, form new friendships, and develop an understanding of the importance of libraries for themselves and their communities.

Maker Literacy: A New Approach to Literacy Programming for Libraries was born out of our shared passion for providing our patrons with the full intrapersonal and interpersonal Maker experience: the physical construction of objects; reflection; and the testing, tweaking, and testing again of their creation, be it the completion of a poem, an artistic masterpiece, a virtual creation on an iPad or tablet, or an interpretive dramatization of a story. Not only are the children filtering the program's activities and information individually; they are also reflecting it back through shared experiences while learning to work together.

Each chapter of this book represents a different type of programming and target audience. Although you might find different disciplines or subjects explored within chapters, literacy is the main focus connecting all of the programs outlined. We present multi-activity programs using the Maker Movement philosophy to enhance all of the 21st-century literacies, including math, art, science, music, traditional language arts, and technology. This holistic approach to learning allows individuals and groups to apply that knowledge in a real-world setting. These types of programs also show children that there are possibilities to be explored beyond what happens in the library.

Many of the programs included in this book use iPads or tablets and, therefore, apps. Where we've suggested specific app titles, we have included a review of the app within the program chapter so that you can best determine whether it works for your program. For your convenience, we've also listed the reviews in the APPendix located at the back of the book for those simply looking to add an app to a program. Further, we recommend the use of many new technologies that you might or might not be familiar with. The Technology Glossary, also found at the back of the book, includes an explanation of these technologies.

The programs in this book are among our favorites. They include themes and activities carefully developed, designed, reflected upon, and fine-tuned. Now they connect us with you: others working with children and sharing our passion for providing them with engaging, fun, creative, and meaningful library programs. The Maker Movement can help kids learn to more fully experience and interact with their world, expressing themselves through words, art, science, technology, math, and performance. These programs cross disciplines, interests, methods, and, thanks to social media websites, physical geography.

Go ahead and *make* these programs your own. Present them exactly as outlined or tweak and tailor them according to your specific needs and audience. Then share them with your patrons (big and small) and watch the learning come full circle. For though librarians are the "teachers," the profound insights kids discover and share in library programs make all of us "students" as well.

eTOTS: AN iPAD OR TABLET STORY TIME FOR CHILDREN AGED TWO TO FIVE

Technology is the future now! Little ones today will be using technology in all facets of their lives—from smart homes to driverless cars. We are *all* living in the midst of a technological revolution. eTots merges traditional story time with technology to give kids a head start. It's a story time that emphasizes teaching two-to-five-year-olds the five literacy skills: talking, singing, reading, writing, and playing. Giving each child/caregiver duo their own iPad or tablet allows both to become comfortable with and learn basic technology skills.

Though technology is the focus of this program, there are many traditional story-time elements as well. For example, this program uses songs, fingerplays, and a simple craft or activity. For each session of eTots, the same basic template or outline is given, with different themes and components inserted. Each program begins with a welcome song and continues with additional songs and fingerplays. To prepare children for the transition to technology, recite the iPad poem next. After exploring two theme-related apps together as a group, at least one of which is a book, allow time for free app play. The program ends with a Maker element, usually a craft or activity.

Prior to the start of the program, load each iPad with the two themed apps and a group of apps for the free app play. It is best to group all the iPad or tablet activities together, and hand out the iPads or tablets just before the technology portion and collect them at its completion. This keeps distraction to a minimum and allows children to concentrate on and derive benefit from the other activities offered.

No matter the theme, the program begins with your favorite opening song. If you can, use a song that welcomes each child individually, by name. Add themed tunes to your most popular story-time songs to create a musical segment. You might wish to choose songs that feature small movements such as hand clapping, toe tapping, or knee slapping rather than songs that feature large movements like jumping, hopping, and parading. If the kids are jumping and hopping, it will be more difficult for them to sit down and focus for the iPad or tablet element. If you are a fan of fingerplays, you might like to mix some in between songs. Or you might wish to include your favorite story-time element: felt board, draw-and-tell story, puppets, and so on.

To prepare for and transition into the technology or iPad or tablet segment of the program, the group recites the following iPad poem, which is based on the nursery rhyme "One, Two, Buckle My Shoe":

> 1, 2 Clean my hands
> 3, 4 Sit on the floor
> 5, 6 Tap the app
> 7, 8 Look, listen, and wait
> 9, 10 Swipe the page
> Now it's time to read again!

In the first line, really clean your hands by wiping them on your clothing. You never know where little hands have been. The second line encourages any of those standing to be seated and ready to receive their iPads or tablets. In the third line, have everyone practice tapping in the air so that the children know what you mean when you tell them to tap the app to open it or to tap an interactive element in the app. In the fourth line, remind the children that they need to listen to the story and other instructions. Swipe in the air during the fifth line to demonstrate what you want the children to do when you ask them to swipe a page to turn it. Now the children will be seated quietly, listening, and ready to receive their iPads or tablets. When handing out the iPads or tablets to the caregiver/child duos, give the iPad or tablet to the child, unless he or she does not wish to take it.

When presenting a book app, read the narration aloud while pointing out the interactive elements. Educational and fun apps require you to begin with simple directions, but then allow users to explore on their own. Walk around the group, ready to answer questions, and try to spot people who seem to need more personalized assistance.

Allow the children to organically transition to the Maker element of the program rather than wrenching the iPad or tablet out of children's hands. Some children will be ready to move to the next activity sooner than others. As the children return the iPads or tablets to you, direct them to the Maker station equipped with supplies you have prepared prior to the program.

Below is an app review list of our eTots participants', big and little, favorite free play apps.

Alphabytes (iOS): Alphabet apps are plentiful, but Alphabytes is a noteworthy example. The pleasingly familiar alphabet cereal motif combined with the happy children voicing the narration provides little ones with a delightful backdrop to the learning exercises. Users are offered the choice of alphabet (actually interactive flashcards), tracing, matching, or spelling activities. The interactive flashcards feature a word beginning with the chosen letter (e.g., arrow for the letter A) and the activity associated with the word. Swiping or tapping the photo-quality graphic of an arrow sets it loose. Underneath the arrow are the words "aim the arrow," letting users know they may press, hold, and turn the bow and arrow in all directions. Tracing provides large, easy-to-use outlines of letters with inner numbered lines for users to trace over with their fingers. Matching asks children to match words, represented by photo-quality graphics of objects, with the first letter of the object's name. Spelling gives users the chance to place the cereal letters into corresponding letter outlines to spell a depicted graphic. This is an alphabet app kids will "eat up."

Dr. Panda's Daycare (iOS and Android): Little ones care for five adorable baby animals in a daycare setting in this role-playing app that encourages creativity. Users may feed their animal babies in the kitchen, play with them outside or inside, put them down for a nap, and so forth. There are more than 1,000 different interactions from which to choose, and each room in the daycare contains clothes, toys, and more for the daycare attendees to utilize. There is no winning (or losing) and no end point for this app. Users are free to explore to their heart's content.

Easy Bake Treats (iOS): Based on the familiar child's toy the Easy-Bake Oven, this app allows users to bake up (and virtually eat, with the chomp of a finger tap) all kinds of delicious goodies. Users choose the item they wish to cook from a familiar list of treats: cupcakes, cake pops, cakes, cookies, pizza, and pretzels. Sorry, no salads here. Children will enjoy adding the ingredients to the bowl, mixing, rolling out, decorating, and taking part in all of the duties of a pint-sized baker. The amount of detail in the graphics and choices creates a realistic kitchen experience for little ones.

Fish School HD (iOS): It is very hard to find an app that is the jack-of-all-trades of early learning, but Fish School HD is just that. Many early-preschool apps that target multiple learning disciplines fall flat on their approach to one or more of them. Fish School HD does not. The graphics, music, and ease of use all combine to help children learn letter recognition, colors, shapes, counting, and spotting differences so effortlessly that they have no idea they are actually learning. Duck, Duck, Moose has created an appealing underwater foray into educational skills for the youngest of app enthusiasts. Users take the plunge in "abc," the first of the categories offered, by listening and watching the school of fish form the letters of the alphabet. A bubble in the left-hand corner offers additional choices: numbers, playtime, shapes, the alphabet song, colors, differences, and matching. In numbers, the fish form the numbers 1 through 20, just as they did in the abcs. Next, it's imaginative playtime with fish and other water creatures. Children may tap on the screen, making the fish larger and faster and sending them to swim around their underwater home. Shapes presents a fish formation of six shapes: circle, oval, triangle, rectangle, diamond, and square. The alphabet song features a school of fish continuously transforming from one letter to the next, while a pleasing songstress intones the classic alphabet song. The song will repeat as many times as the user desires. In colors, users choose one fish that is then joined by a horde of fish friends, all in the same color. In differences, users are asked to find the fish that looks unique. Finally, in the matching section, little ones are asked to use their memory and concentration skills to match fish. Applications for Fish School are now being accepted!

Grandpa's Workshop (iOS and Android): This fix-it-themed app has seven fun mini games and one unique host. Fresh from his workshop, Grandpa is here to encourage users with a dance or a crowd-pleasing high five. Yes, you actually high five Grandpa's hand on the iPad or tablet. The mini games provide practice with numbers, measuring, colors, simple fractions, tool-related vocabulary, and more. The app is targeted for users aged two to six, but the youngest might need assistance with some of Grandpa's puzzles. Interspersed throughout the app are instructional videos featuring real-life craftspeople using the tools shown in the app. Although this app is a favorite with boys, girls will enjoy spending time in Grandpa's Workshop as well.

Lazoo Art Box (iOS): Lazoo, via PBS KIDS, has combined some of their earlier creative art apps and placed them all in one giant art box to fuel any child's imagination and bring out his or her artistic side. Users may choose from any of four art experiences: Let's Squiggle, Let's Color, Let's Draw, or Blank Page. Each section opens with the same quick tutorial. Next, children are given an art prompt, a predrawn picture with something missing that they must complete and written instructions that are highlighted as they are read. A toolbox at the bottom of the screen contains traditional art tools, and some nontraditional ones too (ketchup, anyone?). There are also stickers to add and some ready-made shapes (hearts, snowflakes, pieces of candy, etc.) that may be drawn in lines onto any artistic masterpiece. In Let's Squiggle, youngsters practice prewriting skills by adding squiggles to drawings (e.g., wool to a sheep, smoke to the base of a rocket ship, etc.). They are then directed to press Play and see their drawing come to life. In Let's Color, users practice hand-eye coordination by coloring in simple objects. In Let's Draw, little ones can challenge their imaginations and provide unexpected responses to prompts (e.g., decide what comes out of an elephant's trunk or what hairstyle cartoon friends will be given). In Blank Page, kids are given free rein to express themselves artistically in whatever ways they choose. This engaging, must-have art app gives children a chance to use their imaginations while practicing their prewriting skills and improving their hand-eye coordination. It's an imaginative win-win for preschool artists.

Little Fox Music Box (iOS and Android): Imagine if Richard Scarry made an app featuring classic kids' songs—that's the best way to visualize Little Fox Music Box. The three featured songs, "London Bridge," "Evening Song," and "Old MacDonald Had a Farm," are sung by children and play in the background while users see a scene filled to the brim with interactive elements set in a milieu related to the song. The song lyrics appear at the top of each scene. Of the three, "Evening Song" has the fewest interactive features but uses on-screen designations to point out interactivity. However, because almost all of the elements in "London Bridge" and "Old MacDonald" are interactive, users might not need the tutorial accompanying "Evening Song." A music room is provided where users may make their own tunes using adorable animal and object graphics that play notes or short musical sequences, and a karaoke space allows children to record their own voice set to the songs. For the most bang for your buck, feature "London Bridge" and then allot time for users to explore the other songs at their leisure.

Pepi Doctor (iOS and Android): This app helps take the fear out of a trip to the doctor or dentist by giving children the chance to become little healers and discover what doctors and dentists do. Three ethnically diverse child characters appear for users to treat as their patients. Then, the user will select a pictorial representation of which medical problem they wish to treat: ear infection, cuts, broken bones, dental issues, or a fever. Next, the little doctor is shown his or her patient and presented with a doctor's bag that contains a series of appropriate medical tools, appearing in the order of their use. After each tool is used, the smiling, grateful patient thanks his or her doctor. Once the entire treatment is completed, the little doctor is honored with a round of applause and cheers. This role-playing app might be just the ticket to stress-free doctor visits and, who knows, the app could stimulate an interest in a future career in medicine.

Starring Me in Old MacDonald (iOS): Users will be hard-pressed not to smile, laugh, and cheer as they see themselves interact down on the farm in this customized sing-along presentation of "Old MacDonald Had a Farm." As the app opens, users create their farmer by choosing a photo in their photo library or by taking a photo of anyone or anything they'd like—a stuffed animal, doll, or grown-up—and effortlessly centering it within the head silhouette provided. Next, users may customize their farmer by changing his or her hat, hairstyle, and hair color. Once the farmer is coiffed, he or she is ready to head out to the first of eight interactive musical farm scenes, each corresponding to a verse in the song. Users will see themselves or their "friends" swing on a swing, feed the ducks, play in a mud puddle, play peek-a-boo in the barn, jump on a trampoline at a picnic, drive a truck, visit some hens and, finally, shhh . . . everyone on the farm goes to sleep. Inside the Parents section, the app developers have created a Play and Learn section to help adults get the most out of the app, pointing out all the interactive opportunities for little users. Children will delight as they see themselves or their "friends" count, sort, sing, and move to the rhythm. This personalized app is a surefire hit!

Toddler Email Lite (iOS and Android): This app allows precocious tots to receive emails from any of four nursery-rhyme characters (a 99-cent upgrade to the full version offers email from any of 12 nursery-rhyme characters). The emails are perfectly safe, as they come from within the app itself. Users must "log in" by choosing a pictorial answer to the question of "How's the weather?" Once inside their inbox, children are greeted with the familiar "You've got mail." They can see who the mail is from (e.g., Little Bo Peep, the Sheep, the Muffin Man, or the Muffin) and what the subject heading is (e.g., Count My Cupcakes, Bake a Word, Can You Find Me, etc.). Tapping on the subject heading reveals an email presenting an educational opportunity to practice counting, spelling, or memory skills. They may also tap the Get Email button to receive new messages or the Friends button to see a list of their nursery-rhyme friends. (*Note:* In the lite version, users will see grayed-out icons representing the friends they could have if they upgraded to the paid full version.) This educational app is a fun way to allow little ones to imitate their parents and older siblings and feel big and important too. The free lite version of this app is only available for the iPad. Android users must purchase the full version.

Toddler Toy Factory Free (iOS): After opening the app, users will be presented the choice to Make, Find, or Ship. Choosing Make puts little ones in charge of toy creation. A Seussian-like toy machine appears on the screen. Familiar-looking letter blocks also appear on the screen in random order. Users must insert the letter blocks into the toy machine's intake in the correct order to spell the name of a toy. Above the toy machine intake is a grayed-out version of the letter block that must be inserted first to correctly spell the name of one of 10 toys (the paid version offers 70 toys). Once the letters are properly inserted, the machine spits out the toy, which may then be played with. Until users understand that each grayed-out block atop the intake represents the block that is to be inserted, most little ones will need a bit of grown-up help. In Find, youngsters test their memory and concentration skills by choosing either easy or medium levels of difficulty (the hard level is available only with the paid version) and then matching the toys. Ship provides counting practice as children drag toys into a barrel to pack them for shipping. As each toy is dragged into the barrel, users see the number and hear it counted out. The one negative comes as users must choose between easy or medium levels of difficulty (hard is again available with the paid version only) after each counting screen. This app's activities are the perfect mix of learning (spelling, counting, concentration, memory, and hand-eye coordination) and fun.

Now that your iPads or tablets are filled with free play apps, it's time to consider what each individual session will consist of. Below are three themed suggestions to place in your eTots template.

THEME 1: FROGS

Welcome Song
A selection of songs, fingerplays, or other story-time favorites
iPad Poem
Apps to be shared together as a group:

App Review: Mr. Frog the Neighbor's Dog (iOS)

Tickle your funny bone with this rhyming story designed to elicit laughter. Children will meet a "dog" who isn't really a dog; he's a green frog. Users may choose to have the story read to them or read it themselves. Each page of the story has an interactive element, including a simple animation, coloring, a puzzle, hide-and-seek, and more. Although multiple interactions are presented, each one adds to the story, further engaging the young reader. The hilarious tale ends with the promise of a sequel from one of Mr. Frog's similarly silly friends.

App Review: Rounds: Franklin Frog (iOS)

The first entry in the Rounds series, and a Children's Technology Review Editor's Choice winner, Franklin Frog is an excellent example of a nonfiction app for little ones. Rounds books feature an illustrated animal and all the stages of its life, eventually ending its story where it began: creating a circle of life. This iteration of a Rounds app spotlights the life cycle of a frog. Users are greeted with a choice to "read and play" or "read by myself." Having chosen to be read to, little ones are favored with a clear narration by a child with a charming British accent. The written words are highlighted as they are spoken. Interactions are pointed out by a blinking halo and impart additional frog fun facts matched to Franklin's current environment or activities. Franklin's tongue, so sticky and so long, reminiscent of the printed book *The Icky Sticky Frog* by Dawn Bentley, is bound to be a favorite as users unfurl the frog's tongue to help him eat. Even frog mating is addressed, although in an age-appropriate manner. Soon, Franklin's mate, Felicity, lays eggs and a new generation is born, completing the circle of life. Hakuna matata!

Maker Element: Frog Face Mask with Party Noisemaker Tongue

Locate a frog mask or clipart of the face of a frog online. Prior to the program, print out enough cardstock copies for the kids. Next, cut out the frog faces from the printouts and slash or cut an X on the mouth of the frog. Make the X large enough to insert a party noisemaker. Offer crayons and other art supplies for children to decorate their frogs with. Instruct the caregivers on how to insert the party noisemaker to create the frog's tongue.

THEME 2: SANDRA BOYNTON'S MUSICAL eTOTS

Welcome Song
A selection of songs, fingerplays, or other story-time favorites
iPad Poem
Apps to be shared together as a group:

App Review: Moo, Baa, La, La, La (iOS and Android)

A Children's Technology Review Editor's Choice and Parents' Choice Recommended Pick, the app version of the best-selling book *Moo, Baa, La, La, La* (more than 5 million copies of the print version of the book have been sold) is a crowd-pleasing favorite. Users may choose to read the story by themselves or "have the big guy read it." The app version has the feel of a print book, with realistic page-turning action. The warm and quirky animals featured in the illustrations of the book have been redrawn and recolored to perfection. The words are highlighted as they are read by "the big guy" (the big guy is actually Ms. Boynton's son Keith, who is a very talented narrator). Each animal depicted makes a sound when tapped, and the additional clever interactions add to the unique presentation. From the four spinning pigs on the title page, to the trademark singing-pig trio, to the duck that says "baa" on the final page, children will laugh, learn, and enjoy reading this app, which is truly deserving of the name "interactive book." The only complaint you'll hear is when the book ends, but the conveniently located Start Over button on the final page should take care of that.

App Review: Barnyard Dance (iOS and Android)

Barnyard Dance, based on another Boynton print best-seller, is a sure-to-please winner in the Boynton app arsenal. The app opens with a title page bonus that allows the opportunity for users to tap through the seasons as the scenery behind the book's gathered characters changes to reflect the different times of the year. The users then choose to read the story by themselves or "have the big guy read it." This time, "the big guy" is famed bluegrass musician John Stey, who sounds as if he is calling out directions at a square dance. Just like Moo, Baa, La, La, La, this app features realistic page turning and illustrations that have been redrawn and recolored to perfection. Each page highlights a set of Boynton's signature animal friends who bow, twirl, spin, prance, and promenade with each other in what feels like a square dance of pure joy. It'll be hard to stay seated when this app is done. Dance party, anyone?

Maker Element: Simple Hand-crafted Musical Instruments

Set out all the components for the children and caregivers to create a simple musical instrument. One idea would be to place rice inside an empty single-serving water bottle as a shaker. Provide an assortment of stickers for the children to decorate their shakers with. Break out your favorite tots' playlist and have a toddler dance party!

THEME 3: ROBOTS

Welcome Song
A selection of songs, fingerplays, or other story-time favorites
iPad Poem
Apps to be shared together as a group:

App Review: Pete's Robot (iOS)

You know the old adage: a watched mailbox never receives any mail. This is especially true when you are a blue-haired, stick-figured boy waiting and waiting and waiting, with your trusty dog sidekick, Spot, for Spike the mailmonkey to deliver the robot you ordered online. Users will love Pete, Spot, and their inept but well-meaning robot, Z-123. It seems that when Pete was putting together his robot, he forgot the heartdrive. Without a heartdrive, the robot unwittingly finds himself in quite the pickle. He can't seem to do anything right, but—and it's a big but—he sure can dance! What might be the single best page ever in an interactive book app presents Z-123's participation in a dance-off. Move over, Travolta! After a series of mishaps, the missing heartdrive is discovered and installed and Z-123 is able to save Tony the cat. The robot is a hero, and he and his quirky friends Pete and Spot end the story looking forward to more adventures. Users will be left wanting further adventures as well. Dance on, Z-123!

App Review: Build and Play 3D Planes, Trains, and Robots and More, also known as Build and Play 3D (iOS and Android)

A recipient of The Children's Technology Review Editor's Choice Award, this STEM app for little Makers allows users to put together any of 15 machines (UFO, hot air balloon, Jet Ski, airplane, car, cement mixer, motorbike, ship, train, crane, digger, monster truck, firetruck, and, of course, robots) by sliding the pieces into place, like a puzzle. Attempting to place a piece incorrectly will cause the piece to fly away from the machine being created. The machines are fairly complex for this age group but present a good challenge. Once complete, each machine has a different task or activity for the children to enjoy. Youngsters increase spatial awareness and problem-solving skills while learning the principles of cause and effect as they put together their robots and other machines.

Maker Element: Snap Circuits® or littleBits®, Cubelets® or Robot Stick Puppet

If your library has Snap Circuits or littleBits, you can help children and their caregivers create a project that lights up like Z-123's heartdrive. Easy-to-follow project guides that come with the Snap Circuits or littleBits kits will show you how. (For more information on any of the technological hardware, see the Technology Glossary.)

Owners of Cubelets, magnetic cube-shaped building blocks, can demonstrate how quickly you can assemble a simple robot from Cubelets and allow children and their caregivers to explore the different Cubelet combinations. (For more information, see the Technology Glossary.)

For a low-tech alternative, photocopy robot clipart onto paper to be cut out, decorated, and glued to a craft stick to make a robot stick puppet.

In addition to a story-time technology experience, eTots provides an opportunity for caregivers and children to interact with each other while singing, discussing which apps to play, and creating the Maker element. You may also model behavior for the caregivers by engaging in dialogic reading during the book app, asking the children about the apps they choose to play, and encouraging them to discuss the components of their Maker projects.

2

IT'S NOT JUST FOR KIDS: A PROGRAM FOR CHILDREN AGED FOUR TO SIX AND THEIR PARENTS OR CAREGIVERS TO ATTEND TOGETHER

Four-to-six-year-olds are participating in so many new experiences by themselves—school, sports, dance, and daycare are but a few examples. Sometimes parents feel left out. We've found that when we held programs for this age range, many parents wanted to attend with their children.

In response to this, we developed It's Not Just for Kids, a program for children and their parents or caregivers to attend together. The program template is built around a chosen book title and related projects and activities. It's Not Just for Kids allows you to choose projects that stimulate a child's mind and include more advanced tasks. For example, most four-to-six-year-olds have the mental ability to envision how they want their art to look but lack the manual dexterity to complete a project on their own.

We are not suggesting that parents do the project for their children but instead that librarians model the collaboration of a joint work. Although it might be difficult for some parents to understand that they should allow the children to steer the project, enough gentle reminders will set them on the right path. Another benefit to this program is that parents learn alongside their children and have the opportunity to discuss what they learned both at the library and again at home, creating a new shared interest. Not to mention there are a few extra willing hands to help with clean-up.

SPIN A YARN

The children's author Mac Barnett is a master at spinning yarns, creating complex stories for young and old alike. One of our favorites is *Extra Yarn*, in which a generous young girl finds a box filled with colorful yarn that seemingly has no end. We knew we wanted to design a program around that title, and when we saw the Belgian natural gas commercial "A House That Knits Itself," we knew these two were a match made in heaven. Add in the Paint for Cats app and a wool wet-felting project, and a program was born.

We highly recommend that anyone who works with children, but especially in preparation for this program, watch Mac Barnett's TED Talk entitled "Why a Good Book Is a Secret Door" (www.ted.com/talks/mac_barnett_why_a_good_book_is_a_secret_door). It is too long to show to the parent/child duos, but it is well worth your time. It provides a humorous, honest look at the merging of make-believe and reality and how children are able to suspend belief while reading a book.

Begin your program by reading *Extra Yarn* aloud. Segue into showing the offbeat commercial "A House That Knits Itself" and the separate video depicting the making of the commercial. An online search for the films or a search for the Colossal Art, Design and Visual Culture website should easily produce the film clips. In the clips, after a thermostat switches on, the house appears to knit itself. The objects in the house are covered by knitting, producing a cozy, warm feeling. It's the same feeling that the townspeople in *Extra Yarn* have when given hand-knit sweaters by the main character, Annabelle.

Featured in the commercial is a fascinated feline who observes the knitting process. As a nod to the cat, pass one iPad to each parent/child duo, handing the iPad to the child, and give a guided explanation of the app Paint for Cats. The app is simple and easy to learn, mostly because it is designed for use by actual cats.

App Review: Paint for Cats (iOS)

Fulfill your feline fantasy in this simplistic art app designed for cats but also just right for kids. Users create painted "mousterpieces" (get it?) by batting a mouse with their paws or hands. When the app opens, humans swipe to choose a color palette. Once a palette is selected, a mouse scurries onto the screen. Each time a cat or child taps the mouse, a blob of randomly selected virtual paint from within the palette appears on the screen and a mouse squeaks. The more times the mouse is tapped, the more blobs of paint are added to the artistic creation. Final "mousterpieces" may be shared on Facebook or emailed to friends and family.

The messy part comes next, so be sure to collect all the iPads before moving on to the Maker element: wet felting with wool roving. Rovings are long, thick ropes of raw wool created during the process of making spun yarn, which can be dyed to add color. In the process of wet felting, pieces of the roving are pulled like cotton candy and layered on top of one other. Warm, soapy water is then poured on top of the layers. Agitating the wool, water, and soap allows the fibers of the roving to interlock, creating a very strong fabric. This is also why a wool sweater shrinks, its fibers coming closer together, after being agitated in a warm-water wash cycle.

To introduce children and their grown-ups to this time-consuming process, use this adapted project, which they can complete in a short amount of time, while still learning how fabrics are made. In fabric creation, large pieces of roving are laid out flat between plastic sheeting. Due to time and space limitations, you will not be able to create fabric but

Dry wool roving and wet-felted wool balls happily arranged.

instead will make wet-felted-wool balls that may be turned into jewelry or, if agitated long enough, will become bouncy balls. Below is a list of materials you need to assemble for this program:

- Plastic tablecloths
- Wool roving in assorted colors, available online or in a craft store
- Two medium to large bowls for each table
- Warm and cold water
- Clear dishwashing liquid
- Paper towels (you can never have enough)
- Bubble wrap (optional)
- Small zippered plastic bags (optional)

The instructions to create one wool felted ball are:

- Add one or two drops of the clear dishwashing liquid into the bowl of warm water.
- Tear off small bits of the wool roving, exactly as if you were taking pieces of cotton candy from its stick.
- Repeat this process, alternating colors, stacking the pieces at different angles.
- Press the pieces together until they form a loose ball shape.
- Dip the ball into the bowl of warm, soapy water, as if you were dunking a doughnut into coffee.

- Roll the ball in circles between your hands or between two layers of bubble wrap.
- Periodically redip the ball into the warm, soapy water and continue rolling.
- Eventually, the fibers will interlock and the ball will retain its round shape (this means that fibers will no longer loosen when gently pulled).
- Fully immerse the ball into the bowl of cold water, releasing the soap.
- Blot the wet-felted balls with paper towels.
- For easier transport home, place the balls into the small zippered plastic bags.

Let parents or caregivers know that at home, with a needle or bamboo skewer, they may put a hole in the center of the balls to create beaded, strung jewelry or even a mobile of the solar system.

Spin a Yarn exposes an often-ignored fact: there is a science and artistry behind the fabrics that we wear. Fabrics must be painstakingly designed and created or manufactured. This entire program centers on creating warmth, whether through the knitted sweaters and hat in the book, the natural gas in the commercial, or the comfort in the feel of working with wool. However, the ultimate warmth and comfort comes from the shared interaction between children and their parents or caregivers.

LASCAUX CAVES

Note: This program involves the use of food and/or edible ingredients. Be sure to check ahead with parents and guardians for any food allergies or dietary restrictions. It is your responsibility to adjust the ingredients offered based on the medical needs of the participants in your program.

Lascaux Caves are a series of caves located in France that contain cave paintings more than 17,000 years old. The nonfiction picture book *The Secret Cave: Discovering Lascaux* by Emily Arnold McCully provides an account of the unearthing of the cave paintings considered to be humankind's earliest art. What makes this book more relevant to your patrons is that the cave paintings were uncovered by children playing a game with their dog.

The program begins with a read-aloud of *The Secret Cave: Discovering Lascaux* and a discussion of what has become of the caves following the events of the book. Parents and children will then take part in a simulated Lascaux Cave exploration complete with flashlights. Lastly, participants will create their own cave paintings using materials similar to those available in the Paleolithic Era.

Once you have read *The Secret Cave* to the group, begin your discussion of the erosion of the paintings that quickly halted public access. Talk about the exact replica of the cave paintings that have been painstakingly re-created nearby for tourists, historians, and artists to explore. Then segue to your next activity by telling the attendees that although you wish you could afford to fly everyone to France, instead you will all discover a re-creation of the Lascaux Caves.

To make a simple re-creation of the Lascaux Caves in your program space:

- Before the program, print out a selection of the most iconic images from the caves.

- Tape the printouts around the perimeter of your program area, taking care to position them low enough so that children can easily see them.
- Purchase, borrow, or request that parents bring their own flashlights to the program.
- Warn everyone that you are about to turn out the lights to create a cavelike atmosphere.
- After all the flashlights are on, act as a tour guide as you lead the group through the caves, imparting fun facts as you go.

It is now time for the children and caregivers to create their own original cave paintings. Prehistoric people did not have the luxury of purchasing paints and other art materials at a store but instead gathered their paints from their surroundings: charcoal, soil, food, rocks, and minerals. The supplies you need for naturally sourced Paleolithic-like cave paintings include:

- Jumbo paper lunch bags
- Scissors
- Raspberries to create natural red pigment
- Small disposable bowls
- Plastic forks
- Sketching charcoal to represent burnt sticks
- White chalk simulating ash mixed with animal fat
- Terracotta air-dry clay cut into cubes left to dry as a substitute for soil, rocks, or minerals
- Paper towels, baby wipes, or other hand-cleansing supplies

Several days prior to the program, cut the terracotta-colored clay into cubes and allow to air dry until hardened. This creates a piece of brown chalk that can be used as a writing implement and a less messy substitute for the soil the cavepeople used. For the budget conscious, purchase frozen raspberries and defrost thoroughly before use. Place a portion of the raspberries and a plastic fork for each parent/child duo in one of the disposable bowls. Assemble all of the art materials onto a table and be prepared to explain what each represents to the group.

To begin the cave paintings, instruct the parents to cut off the bottoms of the lunch bags and make a slice up the side, creating a flat piece of brown paper. Ask the children to crinkle the paper and then smooth it so that it lays flat on their work surface. This creates the craggy look of a rock wall.

Encourage the parents to allow the children to choose the subject of the cave paintings and the art materials used. Those who wish to use red pigment should mash the raspberries in the bowl with a fork. The charcoal, white chalk, and terracotta cubes are ready to use as is. Walk around the room, encouraging discussion with the parent/child duos and, when necessary, gently remind parents to let their children do as much as they can on their own.

Optionally, you may add or substitute the Art Set app to create a technological element. The Art Set app allows users to "draw" onto photographs downloaded onto the iPad.

App Review: Art Set (iOS)

Artists of all ages can use this virtual art set, complete with supplies for painting and drawing with an almost unlimited number of art implements (crayons, pencils, oil paints, watercolor paints, pastels, etc.) in an almost unlimited number of ways. Users will be spoiled for choice. Once they select a canvas of different colors and textures and an implement, creation begins. The app boasts virtual pressure sensitivity, making implements easy to use and quick to respond. Five blending tools are provided to customize the look. Users may import photos or images and paint or draw on them. Finished creations may be saved in the iPad's camera roll.

Prior to use, download a set of Lascaux Cave images to each iPad. Look for images that have some drawing but an equal amount of blank space for children to add their own embellishments.

No one knows for sure what the Lascaux Cave drawings represent; they could be stories, instructions, advice, or an expression of worship. Use this program as an opportunity to stimulate conversation, encouraging parents to have a dialogue with their children about what their art means to them.

BOOK YOUR FLIGHT SOON

The Fantastic Flying Books of Mr. Morris Lessmore by William Joyce has all the elements of a perfect literary creation: exciting visuals, heartwarming text, and positive life lessons. It is the quintessential book selection for children and parents to share together because children enjoy the story while adults see beyond to find a roadmap to life. Begin the program with the inspiring film of Aakash Odedra, a dyslexic choreographer who most easily expresses himself through movement. Follow this by using the IMAG-N-O-TRON app to literally bring the print edition of *The Fantastic Flying Books of Mr. Morris Lessmore* to life, and close out the program by placing the parent/child duos in a photographic re-creation of one of the iconic illustrations in the book.

When we watched the TED Talk "Aakash Odedra: A Dance in a Hurricane of Paper, Wind and Light," we had no other thought than "this is the human embodiment of *The Fantastic Flying Books of Mr. Morris Lessmore*." To watch a dancer encircled by a hurricane of paper invokes the plot, illustrations, and spirit of the story. As librarians, knowing that the dancer is dyslexic makes the connection all the more poignant. On a practical note, in order to retain the children's attention and focus, begin showing the talk a minute or so before the papers start to swirl.

To use the IMAG-N-O-TRON app, you must have one copy of *The Fantastic Flying Books of Mr. Morris Lessmore* for each parent/child duo. Without the print version, the app is useless; they are meant to be used together. As the parents read the book with their children, they hold the iPad over each illustration, eliciting a different feature of the app.

App Review: IMAG-N-O-TRON (iOS)

Augmented reality collides with the heartwarming picture book *The Fantastic Flying Books of Mr. Morris Lessmore* to create an awe-inspiring reading experience in the

IMAG-N-O-TRON app. Users must have both a hard copy of *The Fantastic Flying Books of Mr. Morris Lessmore* and the IMAG-N-O-TRON app. When the app opens, users choose to "play" and then hold the iPad steadily over each page. The app will read the text of the page to the user and, at the same time, the static illustrations on the pages will come to life. Users will receive a clue when it is time to "look up." That's when the real fun begins. Animations and illustrations from the book and sound effects are projected onto the walls and objects in the very room users are in. In this case, the cliché is true; the book *The Fantastic Flying Books of Mr. Morris Lessmore* literally comes to life with the addition of the IMAG-N-O-TRON app.

Now you will provide parents and children with an opportunity to do something they've always dreamed of—be in the pages of a treasured book. Re-create one of the pages of the book on the floor of the program room. We chose the scene of the lovely lady, who we suspect is a librarian, floating through the sky suspended by ribbons attached to flying book balloons. In our photographs, the parent/child duos took the place of the lovely lady. You can create this scene by using items you most likely already have on hand. We used the following:

- Three or four sky-blue plastic tablecloths
- A selection of popular children's books
- An assortment of colorful ribbon
- Clear plastic tape
- Ladder
- Camera, iPad, or other photographic device
- White poster board
- Cotton balls
- Glue

In the interest of time, prepare your tableau prior to the program. To do this, you should:

- Make simple cotton-ball clouds by cutting cloud shapes out of the poster board and gluing cotton balls on top.
- Lay down the plastic tablecloths and tape the seams to join them.
- In order to avoid a reflection from the tape in the final photographs, flip the joined tablecloths tape-side down.
- Create book balloons by taping ribbons to the back covers of the children's books.
- Lay the book balloons onto the tablecloths at a variety of heights as if you were creating a balloon bouquet.
- Position the ladder next to the tableau.
- Use two volunteers to figure out the optimal placement of the participants, book balloons, clouds, and ladder as seen through your photographic device.

Remind the participants of the illustration you chose to depict from the book. Invite each pairing to pose within the "page" as you snap a treasured memory. If you have enough staff and the budget for colored ink, print out the photographs as they happen. If not, do what we did; post them on social media websites and allow parents to print them themselves. (*Note:* Remember to obtain written permission before posting any photos that include images of participants onto social media websites.)

For many people, finding *that* book begins a lifelong love of reading. Just like Morris's lovely lady, librarians should strive to be the connection to that literary catalyst igniting the process.

There are times when it is best for children to attend programming by themselves to encourage independence, socialization, and the development of critical thinking. However, It's Not Just for Kids or any program that parents or caregivers and children attend together offers benefits as well. Parent/child events encourage participants to see the library as a place the whole family can enjoy together. It also presents the opportunity for special one-on-one time for parents with more than one child.

3

USE YOUR WORDS: MULTI-ACTIVITY PROGRAM FOR EMERGING READERS AGED FOUR TO SIX TO REINFORCE BASIC LITERACY SKILLS USING TECHNOLOGY, ART, AND FILMMAKING

Children between the ages of four and six show a marked interest in reading and writing words. They want to be able to write their names and have others be able to read it. It's the first step on their way toward being able to communicate clearly to people other than their siblings, parents, or caregivers. Use Your Words encourages children to practice the literacy skills necessary to communicate effectively in a variety of ways: linguistically, kinesthetically, verbally, and visually.

The best activities to reinforce these skills contain a combination of focus and abandon. Programs incorporating technology, art, and drama provide children with different avenues of self-expression, communication, and playful learning. They will be having so much fun, they won't even realize they are hard at work developing the literacy skills they need.

YOU'VE GOT MAIL!

Even in this technological world of instant messaging, kids still love to send and receive letters through the mail. Learning to write a letter is an important skill that they will use throughout their lives. No matter the medium you send your messages through, they need to be presented in a clear and concise manner.

To make learning the parts of a letter more fun, this program follows Alfie, an alligator in Jennifer E. Morris's early reader *Please Write Back!*, who writes a letter to his grandmother and eagerly awaits her reply. After sharing the story aloud, the group will create a simple letter together, explore the Dr. Panda Mailman app, and the children will create and mail their own personalized postcards.

Before registration, make or buy a set of postcards, one for each child. If you already own cardstock and wish to save money, you may create your own postcards following the guidelines from the United States Postal Service, which can be found online: http://pe.usps .com/text/qsg300/Q201.htm.

Hand out these postcards upon registration. Explain to parents that the children will be writing postcards that will be mailed at the conclusion of the program. It is important that the child choose to whom the postcard will be sent so they will be more invested in the project. Caregivers should address the postcards, writing in both the "to" and "from" addresses, and bring them to the program. You also need to purchase the stamps.

As part of the program, you will be "mailing" the letters. If your library has a mailbox on site, as ours does, it's simply a matter of a walk to the mailbox. If your library does not have a mailbox on site, you might wish to create and decorate a cardboard box to look like a mailbox to collect the letters to be mailed at a later time. Ideally, a quick phone call to your local civic-minded post office might produce a volunteer letter carrier who would be willing to come to your program, provide a short talk about their job, and collect the postcards.

Open the program with a read-aloud of *Please Write Back!* While reading the story, encourage the children to share their thoughts on Alfie's feelings and their own experiences sending and receiving mail. Drag out a piece of paper onto which the group can write a letter from an easel or project from a computer or tablet. Explain and point out the parts of the letter as you go: greeting, body, closing or salutation, and signature.

Hand out the iPads or tablets and explore the Dr. Panda's Mailman app together. Allow a reasonable amount of time for the children to use the app individually.

App Review: Dr. Panda's Mailman (iOS and Android)

The series of apps carrying the Dr. Panda name are open-ended role-playing apps that provide hours of fun and a variety of experiences for their young users. Dr. Panda's Mailman allows would-be letter carriers to experience a day in the life of their mail delivery person. The day begins in the post office, where users opt for either a package to be filled with a chosen toy or to create and decorate a postcard. After designating one of the 10 animals from the animal recipient board and selecting one of four areas (mountain, village, forest, or fields) in which to deliver their mail, Toto the tortoise weighs the package or postcard and licks a stamp to be placed on top of it. Dr. Panda mounts his scooter and rides off, traversing the various roads, performing scooter tricks, pushing through boxes, and shooing away birds while delivering users' packages to their grateful recipients. Once one delivery is made, the process starts over again with a customized new adventure for Dr. Panda Mailman.

Once the time for app exploration has elapsed, hand out the postcards to the children. The "from" address will help you match each postcard to the correct child. Tell the children they may draw pictures, write, or both; it is their postcard to send. Walk around the room answering any questions the children might have. Be sure to keep in mind that at this age spelling and grammar need not be corrected unless a child specifically asks. The point of this program is for children to enjoy the process of creating and sending a letter.

As they finish their letters, invite the children to come up and choose a stamp and help them affix it to the front of their postcards. Consider drawing a square in the upper right-hand corner to help guide stamp placement. Now is the time for the children to mail their postcards in whatever manner works best for you.

In You've Got Mail!, children also learn that in order to receive a letter, sometimes you need to write and mail one first. Just like Alfie in *Please Write Back!*, we hope the children will enjoy the fruits of their labor when they receive a reply.

ALPHABET MASH-UP

There are so many great ways to teach the letters of the alphabet to children; why choose just one? We've mashed together our favorites to create a fun mix of traditional and technological educational tools designed to meet the needs of all learners.

This program begins with the traditional activity of creating a group story using flashcards and Post-it® Notes. Technology takes over when the children explore the alphabet art app Drawnimal, learn letter identification and spelling with the Words for Osmo app, and practice sound blending with the MaKey MaKey Classic®. End the program with a traditional Maker element—a craft project related to the group story.

Before the program, go online and find a themed set of flashcards featuring simple words and pictures. We chose a set of farm flashcards featuring a farmer, barn, tractor, and an assortment of animals, but you may choose whichever theme you prefer. If you wish, you may create your own set of themed flashcards. Be sure to include pictures for those children not yet able to read. Right before the program, lay out the flashcards on the floor of your program area so that all flashcards are visible.

To begin Alphabet Mash-up, explain to the children that you will be writing a story together using the words on the flashcards. One at a time, invite the children to take one or two flashcards and create a sentence for the story. Write every word or punctuation mark of each sentence not included on a flashcard on a single Post-it® Note. Adhere the Post-it® Notes and flashcards in sentence order on the floor. Read the sentence aloud, pointing to the words on the Post-it® Notes and flashcards as you go. Repeat the process with each child, reading the cumulative story aloud each time, until every child has had a turn. Read the complete story following the last child. An exercise of this sort reinforces sentence structure, use of punctuation, word recognition, and the concept of a story as a progression of ideas.

After a traditional story-writing activity, you can transition to the technological portion of our program. Begin by seating the children at tables preset with paper and pencils. Hand each child an iPad loaded with the Drawnimal app. The Drawnimal app combines art with letter recognition.

App Review: Drawnimal (iOS)

This animated alphabet app distinguishes itself from the hordes of others with its creative flair. Children lay an iPad onto a piece of paper larger than the iPad, keep a writing instrument at the ready, and open the app. Choosing a letter of the alphabet brings up an unfinished drawing of an animal whose name begins with that letter. Users are visually instructed to complete the animal by drawing the finishing touches onto the paper. For example, the letter "b" brings up a drawing of a bear. He is missing his ears. Youngsters must draw the ears onto the paper above the iPad so that the bear can hear. Once done, they may tap the green arrow or Play button and be rewarded with an animation. The now eared bear gives a loud growl. Drawnimal provides users with a happy blend of the technological and the traditional.

If your kids respond like ours, it will be hard to move them away from the Drawnimal app, but once they experience the Words for Osmo app, they will be glad they did. The Words for Osmo app only requires one iPad for the entire group. Children will reinforce the skills in both the Post-it® Note story and the Drawnimal app, with the addition of trying their hands at spelling. Choose the easiest level. We had each child line up and take a turn, enlisting the help of those waiting if needed. However, you might decide to make this element into a game show and give sticker rewards to those children correctly identifying letters to spell words.

App Review: Words for Osmo (iOS)

Teach letter recognition, spelling, and build vocabulary with the simple word-guessing game using the letter tiles included in the Osmo® kit and the free Words for Osmo app. Users open the app and choose I Spy, Junior Learning Words, or Custom. They can then opt for Versus (against a friend) or Zen (any number of players). As the game begins, a picture appears on the iPad screen along with the direction "guess this word." A colored circle is filled with the letters comprising the word. One of the circles is blank. It is the user's mission to find the correct letter among the letter tiles and place it in front of the iPad (in the range of the Osmo kit's reflective device mounted on the iPad's camera). Any incorrect guess will be shown at the top of the screen. Users are provided with a generous but limited number of incorrect guesses. Registering online for an Osmo account allows users to upload their own photos and create a list of sight words, spelling words, and so on. This child-appropriate take on Hangman will make learning _un!

Our next activity uses a MaKey MaKey Classic and focuses on an additional skill—sound blending. Children touch different letters on a printout of sound-blending equations and hear themselves creating the sound of the letters. Alternatively, if you prefer, you may record the sound of the letters before the program and allow the children to listen to you voicing the sound blends. Your choice will depend on how much time you have allotted and/or how interactively you wish to teach the technology. If you choose to use the MaKey MaKey Classic sound-blending exercise, you will need:

- MaKey MaKey Classic
- Laptop
- One sheet of white copy paper
- Scissors
- Aluminum foil
- Tape

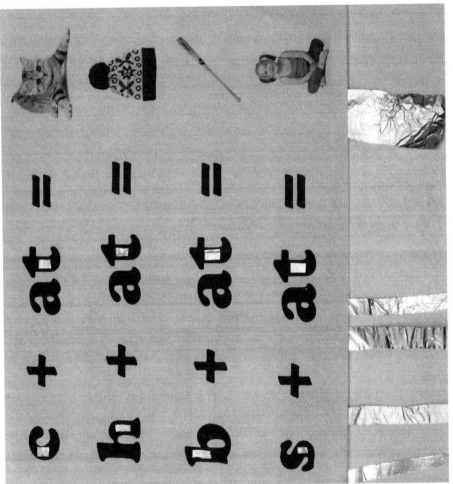

Front view of sound-blending printout.

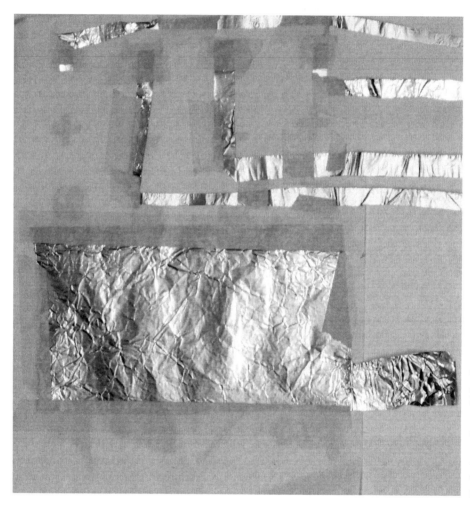

Back view of sound-blending printout.

Before the program, begin by drafting simple sound equations (e.g., c + at = cat). Feel free to copy the example used in our program from the accompanying photo or print out your own. Cut one small hole in each of the letters and sound blends to the left of the equals sign. On the back of the printed copy paper, tape thin strips of aluminum foil, beginning each strip slightly above the hole and allowing the foil to continue past the bottom edge of the printout. You will only need one strip of foil for the sound blends "at." Referencing the photo will clarify this process.

Create a Scratch code for the sound-blending equation at the Scratch website. Scratch is a user-friendly, online programming tool presented by the Massachusetts Institute of Technology. Scratch allows users to program and share animations, games, and stories. The Scratch code required features repetitions of the brown Events Scratch block and the fuchsia Sound Scratch block with different values inserted in the drop-down menus. In the code below, the phrase "when (_____) key pressed" should be inserted via the brown Events Scratch block onto the Scratch scripts area, choosing from the drop-down menu the phrases in parentheses below. The phrase "play sound (__)" should be inserted via the fuchsia Sound Scratch block, again choosing from the drop-down menu the letters and symbols in parentheses below.

    when (left arrow) key pressed
    play sound (c)

    when (up arrow) key pressed
    play sound (h)

    when (right arrow) key pressed
    play sound (b)

    when (down arrow) key pressed
    play sound (s)

    when (space) key pressed
    play sound (at)

Practice recording in Scratch to familiarize yourself with the process. Connect the MaKey MaKey Classic to the laptop via the directions provided by the MaKey MaKey Quick Start Guide (at the time of this publication located at http://makeymakey.com/howto.php). Following the directions at the MaKey MaKey Quick Start Guide and using the Scratch coding as a guide, connect the alligator clips to both the MaKey MaKey Classic and the appropriate aluminum foil strips.

If you've prerecorded your own voice, when you press the foil showing through the hole in the letters on the printout, you should hear your recording of the sound of that letter or blend. Moving your finger across the equation quickly should blend the sounds to form the word. The same process applies to recording the children's voices, but budget extra time to do so. Not only will having the children record the sounds of the letters and blends reinforce the concept, it is just plain fun for the kids to hear what their voices sound like.

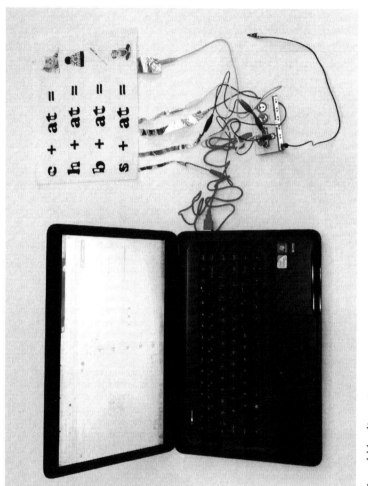

Sound-blending set up.

End the program on a traditional note with a Maker element related to the theme of your flashcard story. Our project reflected the farm theme. We presented the children with a coloring sheet of a barn featuring a prominent open barn door. On paper cut to fit in the barn-door opening, children will draw a farm animal. You may choose to give the children multiple squares of precut paper to create a variety of farm animals or print out a selection of clipart farm animals for them to color.

After coloring in the barn, children place their farm animals in the barn-door opening. You can then give each child two Post-it® Notes and instruct them on how to place the Post-it® Notes onto the coloring sheet over the animals to create doors that open and close. You might wish to sing a rousing version of "Who's in the Farmhouse" (to the tune of "Who Let the Dogs Out?"), having each child take a turn filling in the lyrics with their animal's sound. For example, everyone sings "Who's in the Farmhouse?" to which a chosen child responds, "Oink, oink, oink." The remaining children guess which farm animal it is.

Alphabet Mash-up presents a variety of letter-learning activities in a constant stream. You set the pace, but allow the children's responses to each of the elements to be your guide. You may move the children along individually or as a group; if you choose, children enjoying one activity may remain until they are ready to move to the next. This inherent flexibility allows for a program you can tailor on the spot to meet the specific needs of your group.

ACTION: TAKE THREE

Filmmaking is a unique way of teaching and reinforcing literacy skills. Most children love seeing themselves on camera and in the spotlight. This series of programs—designed to be performed together, although they may be presented individually—offers the opportunity for participants to shine while learning new skills.

If you choose to offer Action: Take Three as presented, you will create three individual films, each focusing on a different set of literacy skills and using a different technique. *Build-a-Word* teaches and reinforces sound blends and word construction with stop motion animation. *Shhhh!* focuses on visual literacy, nonverbal storytelling skills, and sequencing by transforming any picture book into a silent film. *Sound Effects* heightens the participants' listening skills, increasing communication abilities and encouraging active hearing, which helps children to process what is being said. You might wish to share one or all of the final films on your library's social media websites. (*Note:* Remember to obtain written permission before posting any videos including images of participants onto social media websites.)

Build-a-Word

Words are created by blending different sounds together (e.g., s + it = sit). Stop motion animation blends still photographs together to create a movie. The two processes go hand in hand in this, the first of our theatrical trio of programs.

For this activity, you will photograph children within the Stop Motion Studio app, holding poster board to visually represent the sounds and sound blends of letters coming together to create a word.

App Review: Stop Motion Studio (iOS and Android)

Almost anyone can make a stop motion film using the Stop Motion Studio app. A welcome video greets users to explain the process of creating a stop motion film or animation. A small number of easy-to-use controls guide the process. Future filmmakers point and shoot still photographs that the app strings together to create a film. An overlay and grid help users maintain continuity between shots. Editing takes place within the app using the familiar tools of cut, copy, and paste. Films may be enhanced with music from an iTunes library or users may insert on-the-spot vocal narration. The in-app purchase feature pack adds a variety of extra elements and is worth the price. For the best results, you may wish to purchase tripods to steady those excited hands on the brink of creation. Completed cinematic creations may be posted online to social media websites directly through the app. If the children appear in the films, remember to obtain written permission before posting any videos onto social media websites.

Before the program begins, assemble a list of words that may be broken into two parts. Keep the words as simple as possible, choosing words composed of three or four letters. Write each of the parts of the words individually on sturdy pieces of poster board. Following the example s + it = sit, write the letter "s" on one piece of poster board and "it" on another. Bring up a duo of children and show them the word as a whole, explaining that it is made up of parts.

Pair the children and assign a word to the first duo. Then, ask the children what their assigned word means. If necessary, provide them with the definition, as they will be acting out the word in part of the film. Give each child in the duo one piece of poster board, representing one part of the word. Ask the children to stand approximately three feet apart. Photograph the duo with the Stop Motion Studio app, incrementally moving the children toward each other while the remaining children watch. Once they are standing beside each other, they move their poster boards together to fully form the word. Take several photos of the children in each position to create the illusion of waiting a beat to allow the viewer to fully comprehend the word. Instruct the children to then act out the word as you photograph them. This stop motion animation smoothly represents the creation, sounding out, and personification of a simple word.

For example, when filming a stop motion animation of the word "jump," begin your film with two children standing three feet apart. One child would hold a piece of poster board with a "j" on the front. The other child would hold a separate piece of poster board with "ump" written on the front. Take at least four photographs of the children in this original position using the Stop Motion Studio app. Instruct the children to take one small step closer to each other, but remain facing the photographer. Take at least four photographs of this second position. Continue this process until the children are standing next to each other. Photograph the children holding their pieces of poster board together, completing the word. Take at least 16 photographs of this position in order to provide a waiting period in which the viewer processes the word. Ask the children to act out the word by jumping up and down while you take multiple photographs. Repeat the process with the remaining children, choosing a new word for each duo until all the children have a starring role in their animation.

Shhhh!

Choose your favorite picture book, keeping in mind that you will need a number of characters to accommodate parts for all of the children in your group. Not every part needs to be large. Simply allow each child his or her moment on screen. Don't worry about complicated sets or costumes; what is important is children learning to portray a character's actions and emotions within an ordered story. You may capture the children's expressive journeys on film with the Silent Film Studio app or by simply recording the children on an iPad or tablet, smartphone, or camera.

> **App Review: Silent Film Studio (iOS)**
>
> Anyone can easily create a fabulous looking, old-time silent movie with the Silent Film Studio app. The app allows users to create their films from photos on an iPad camera roll or video clips shot within the app or located in the iPad's library. Users customize their movie's theme, title cards, and music. Editing works simply with a straightforward drag and drop. A red curtain appears when users wish to play their film in the app so that each showing of any silent film opens with a flourish. The end result is polished with an authentic nod to the silent film era.

Begin this program by sharing the picture book together as a group. If you choose to use the Silent Film Studio app, you might wish to base your program on Mo Willems's book *That Is Not a Good Idea*, which has a silent film motif. You can edit your movie within the app. For those filming without an app, we suggest Bill Thomson's *Chalk* because of its kid appeal in topics: dinosaurs, playgrounds, sidewalk chalk art, and the richness in variety of expression and action. If you choose to film without an app, it is likely that you will have to edit your movie with your choice of movie-editing software.

Once everyone is familiar with the story, assign a character to each of the children. Rehearse the book, either page by page or just hitting the highlights, depending on the number of children in your program. When ready, film the children reenacting the picture book, one page or section at a time, stopping and restarting filming with each new section. If you choose *That Is Not a Good Idea*, the text of the book may be entered as is onto the title cards in the Silent Film Studio app.

If using the Silent Film Studio app, view the newly created silent film as a group for the final element of the program. Then, practice sequencing by reordering the film segment clips and asking the children for their help in putting the film back together in the proper order. Show each attempt as a film so that children can see if they have incorrectly sequenced any of the film segment clips.

If you are not using the app, edit the film in your choice of software in front of the children. You may employ the same technique of reordering the clips and asking the children to correctly sequence them. Unless you are already familiar with your chosen movie-editing software, this might take a bit more time than editing within the app. Conclude your program with another viewing of the film in its proper order.

Sound Effects

Sound plays a very important role in a movie. It helps reveal the mood, set the tone, and tell the story. Sound is also a key element in letter identification and word creation. Any story can be enjoyed on its own, but adding sound effects enhances the experience. This activity allows participants to explore different sounds and how those sounds help in story progression. It also encourages active listening and immersive participation.

Everyday objects can create movie-quality sound effects that may be recorded within a story using a camera, an iPad or tablet, a smartphone, or a webcam. For example, a piece of poster board shaken vigorously creates the sound of thunder, rhythm sticks beaten on a carpet emulates the sound of rain hitting a roof, and verbal hissing creates the illusion of the presence of a snake. These three sound effects, or any others, may be used to begin the program. Instruct the children to close their eyes while you create one of the sounds above (or your own sound effect) and ask the children to guess what they think the sound effect is.

After a few rounds of the guessing game, put out an assortment of everyday objects whose sounds the children can explore. Anything capable of making a sound, either independently or with the help of another object, will work; for example, a pen rubbed across the side of a ribbed water bottle could create the purr of a cat. Allow time for children to explore many sound effects and then choose a favorite.

Once their favorites have been chosen, gather the children together to write a story incorporating all of their sound effects. Include at least one sentence that features the sound effects of each child. If you are feeling especially ambitious, help the children write a cumulative tale that offers multiple opportunities for each child. This story will become the script for your film. The next part of the program will be tricky to accomplish alone. Enlist a parent volunteer, older sibling, or staff member to either film the children creating their sound effects within the story as you narrate the story or have them narrate as you film. There are multiple ways to film this program. You may choose to show the narrator, to focus only on the children, highlighting them as they create their sound effects, or a combination of both. Pick the method and filming device that works best for you.

Action: Take Three allows children to use a preponderance of their senses to tell a story. These activities create a deeper understanding of stories and storytelling while allowing children to express themselves more completely and increasing their ability to listen and comprehend.

There is a misconception that literacy is the ability to read and write. It's just not that simple. Children need to develop letter recognition and fine motor skills in order to become literate. Once they can read and write, they need to figure out the nuances within reading and writing and how different people react to the spoken and written word. By practicing many ways to communicate, children will become more well-rounded and able to give and receive information in multiple ways. This turns limited possibilities into unlimited options and promotes future personal and professional successes.

4

ROOKIE READERS 2.0: BOOK DISCUSSION, APP EXPLORATION, AND ART WORKSHOP FOR CHILDREN AGED FIVE TO SIX

A book discussion group for upper-elementary-age students is a library staple. However, many librarians have never considered offering a book discussion group for five- and six-year-olds. There are books geared specifically for emergent readers that seem to be ripe for a book discussion group. Choosing the right book and offering it up for discussion might lead to a revelatory experience for both the group leader and the children and will help foster a love of reading within the group.

Rookie Readers 2.0 is a monthly book discussion group, app exploration, and art workshop for children aged five and six. One book is selected for each session, upon which all the activities are based. Interlibrary loan enough copies so that each attendee may borrow his or her own book upon registration and return it on program day. This will ensure that the children will be given ample time to read the book and/or have it read aloud to them by a grown-up. Therefore, they will arrive at the program familiar with the story and ready to participate.

In this chapter, you will find three of our favorite Rookie Readers 2.0 program templates. These books were chosen for their interplay of text and visuals, appealing graphics and illustrations, natural extensions to activities and literary elements, and the ease with which children relate to the main characters. You can surely think of many more books that would be just the right fit for this program and your participants.

I JUST NEED A LITTLE SPACE

Everyone needs a space to call their own. It be a bedroom, a corner desk, or a comfy chair: a physical and mental space where you feel safe and free to relax and let your dreams and imagination soar. In Eileen and Marc Rosenthal's picture book *I'll Save You Bobo!*, Willy and his stuffed monkey, Bobo, are simply trying to find a quiet and private place to write and illustrate a picture book starring Bobo. But Earl the cat has other plans as he repeatedly interrupts and thwarts their progress, leaving readers and listeners to wonder if their efforts will ever come to fruition.

I Just Need a Little Space allows kids to reclaim a spot all their own. After reading the story aloud, as a nod to Earl, participants will play with the Paint for Cats app. Then they will each construct a tent with chairs and blankets, just as Willy and Bobo did, and retreat inside their dwellings with paper and crayons to draw the further adventures of Willy, Bobo, and, perhaps, even Earl.

Upon registration, give each child a copy of the book that you have acquired via interlibrary loan. Encourage him or her to bring along a favorite stuffed animal friend with whom to share the experience and possibly become the subject of their own picture book.

We've all experienced the powerlessness of unexpected distractions and interruptions. Young readers and listeners will easily identify with Willy's need and search for a place for quiet creation and reflection. A read-aloud of *I'll Save You Bobo!* will elicit examples from the children of their own pets' antics and provide a natural transition to the Paint for Cats app.

App Review: Paint for Cats (iOS)

Fulfill your feline fantasy in this simplistic art app designed for cats but also just right for kids. Users create painted "mousterpieces" (get it?) by batting a mouse with their paws or hands. When the app opens, humans swipe to choose a color palette. Once a palette is selected, a mouse scurries onto the screen. Each time a cat or child taps the mouse, a blob of randomly selected virtual paint from within the palette appears on the screen and a mouse squeaks. The more times the mouse is tapped, the more blobs of paint are added to the artistic creation. Final "mousterpieces" may be shared on Facebook or emailed to friends and family.

This program offers a two-part Maker element: tents the children design and build themselves and picture books they write and illustrate inside their tents. Days before the program, bring in blankets and sheets, either your own or borrowed from staff and friends. On the day of the program, pile the folded blankets and sheets in the back of your program area, along with a selection of chairs and tables. Place an assortment of paper, crayons, and hardcover books or clipboards to be used as work surfaces onto an art supply table.

Allow the children time to position the chairs and tables into tents, forts, or other arrangements of their choosing, and then cover their spaces with the blankets and sheets. Once finished, they may crawl inside with the paper, crayons, a sturdy work surface, and perhaps a favorite stuffed animal and draw and create without the fear that Earl, or anyone else, will be making an unwanted appearance any time soon.

I Just Need a Little Space provides multiple jumping-off points for librarians interested in changing up the program. Sample components to modify include the creative process of writers, illustrators, and picture book production; an introduction to architecture; or as a story-time addition to the theme of camping, as Willy and Bobo have done in their jungle adventure. No matter the direction you choose, it's best to keep in mind that although alone time is a necessity, it's always nice to return to the ones we cherish—even Earl.

YOU MUST BE THIS TALL TO RIDE

No matter your age or height, boarding and riding the roller coaster of life means occasionally having to try something new. Marla Frazee's book *Roller Coaster* captures the reactions and emotions universal to the experience of new undertakings—in this case, a ride on the roller coaster The Rocket. Though the story centers on one little girl, her fellow passengers are undergoing their own exploits as they careen their way through the ups, downs, and loop de loops of their adventures. (*Note:* Remember to interlibrary loan enough copies for each participant prior to your program.)

Musician and author Jim Gill opened our program with the song "My Ups and Downs" followed by a read-aloud of *Roller Coaster*. Participants then explored the app SpinArtX and acted out another silly Jim Gill tune, "I Took a Bath in the Washing Machine." For a Maker element, the kids designed their own roller coasters with poster board, markers, pom-poms, and magnets.

Begin the event with a discussion of amusement parks—the sights, the sounds, and the different types of rides to be enjoyed. To re-create the excitement of a roller coaster, play Gill's "My Ups and Downs" from his CD entitled *Jim Gill Sings Do Re Mi on His Toe Leg Knee*. Start by having everyone bend at their knees and touch their fingertips to the floor, then reach and stretch up and down again and again as the song directs. For a second playing of the song, invite all the participants to line up one behind the other. Lead the line forward around the room in large, sweeping circles, up and down, mimicking a ride on The Rocket. At the song's end, everyone will be seated and ready to listen to a retelling of Frazee's *Roller Coaster*.

Amusement parks not only feature vertical rides like roller coasters and Ferris wheels but also spinning rides such as carousels and teacups. To create a spinning experience for the participants, extend the amusement park atmosphere with the SpinArtX app.

App Review: SpinArtX (iOS)

SpinArtX allows users to easily generate their own glowing creations. Users choose from 54 individual colors or a rainbow effect to swirl shapes using either dotted or straight lines. In spin mode, swiping the screen accelerates the movement of the design. With a swirl of their fingers in view mode, users can see their object from all angles. The intuitive interface makes for a user-friendly experience. Though the app offers only one activity, if the program is not centered on the app alone, it makes a fine choice.

If you do prefer spin over height, you'll love another Jim Gill favorite, "I Took a Bath in the Washing Machine," from his work *Jim Gill Sings the Sneezing Song and Other Contagious Tunes*, and so will the kids. This song is the perfect segue into the program's Maker element, designing a roller coaster using simple household materials:

- White poster board
- Scissors
- Small, round magnets (available for purchase online and in craft stores)
- Pom-poms

- Glue
- Markers

Before the program, cut the poster board into 12-inch squares. Glue one pom-pom to the top of half of the magnets and allow the glue to dry; these magnets represent the person experiencing the ride. Place the poster board, magnets, and markers onto an art table.

Children will use the markers to draw their own version of The Rocket, their favorite amusement park ride, or a wished-for structure from their own imaginations. Once satisfied with their work, they may take one magnet with a pom-pom and place it on top of their poster board at the start of the ride. Match up another magnet under the poster board so the two magnets are "touching" through the poster board. Moving the magnet underneath the poster board will pull the top magnet along the ride's track and simulate a passenger enjoying all the thrills and excitement the ride can offer.

Marla Frazee is masterful at pairing sparse, understated prose with energetic and detailed illustrations and visual extensions. Readers will find many smaller stories within the pictures and, like the little girl who wishes to ride The Rocket again "right now!," will continue to discover many more with the repeated readings they will surely ask for. You Must Be This Tall to Ride provides all the fun of a day at the park without the sunburn, long lines, and high cost of snacks and parking.

ANY MORE QUESTIONS?

Kids feel as though they are constantly being asked the same questions over and over again but don't always have the words to express their answers fully. When Grandma fires questions about school at her granddaughter in Hanoch Piven's picture book *My Best Friend Is as Sharp as a Pencil and Other Funny Classroom Portraits*, she decides to show Grandma the answers in the form of collage portraits made from common household objects. Any More Questions? provides participants with an exercise in wordplay and the chance to create thoughtful and meaningful works of art, while at the same time allowing you to clean out your craft closet or junk drawer.

This program offers the perfect setting for a lesson on similes: figures of speech comparing two unrelated objects or concepts, usually through connecting words (e.g., *like* or *as*). A great example is this month's Rookie Readers 2.0 selected title, *My Best Friend Is as Sharp as a Pencil*. After listening to the story read aloud, children will make their own virtual object collage portraits with Hanoch Piven's app, Faces iMake. The session concludes with the participants creating collage portraits using traditional art supplies and unused objects and trinkets found throughout the library and/or raided from personal junk drawers.

My Best Friend Is as Sharp as a Pencil and Other Funny Classroom Portraits poses a series of questions from Grandma about her granddaughter's school. Where one page literally answers a question with a list of similes and icons of found objects, a turn of that page reveals a spread of the same objects rearranged into a composition that fully brings the subject of the answer to life. Because children read the interlibrary loaned book at home (or have it read to them) before the program, they are free to pore over the collages and produce responses to the very same questions they are frequently asked about *their* school experiences. An end note from the author further encourages readers to start making collages of their own, giving children another outlet for creative expression.

A read-aloud of the story opens the program with listeners excitedly sharing the names of the people in response to Grandma's questions. Piven has also created the Faces iMake app, an extension of his collective works and a natural transition to virtual collage portrait making by the children.

App Review: Faces iMake (iOS)

Hanoch Piven's right-brain creativity app opens with a video tutorial that presents users with a guide to creating their own Piven-inspired collages. Five additional video lessons are also available to view. Users may begin by choosing a colored face shape and then add objects from different categories, such as candy, music, toys, and food, to fill in the features on their face as demonstrated in the first lesson, or they may start by creating a design all their own. The app comes loaded with a special Faces iMake song that plays continuously in the background. Users may also add songs from iTunes or silence the sound altogether. An inspirational gallery of art created by the Piven family is provided. Designs may be shared via email or placed in the user's camera roll. Faces iMake nurtures the creative instinct in every child and provides a pleasurably satisfying outlet for self-expression that is both stimulating and entertaining.

It is now time for the children to create picture collages from a variety of traditional art supplies and found or recycled objects; the children's portraits will be as unique as the supplies and objects you have on hand. Before the program, place squares of construction paper or poster board, crayons, markers, glue, and any found or recycled objects onto the art supply table. (We have found this type of program to be a great way to make use of leftover summer reading incentives that are taking up way too much storage space!) Though the kids may make portraits of teachers or classmates from school, they are of course free to create a portrait of anyone they wish—a parent, friend, pet, or even themselves.

Children aged five and six are at the perfect stage to begin attending a regularly scheduled book discussion group. They are ready to accept the responsibility of caring for a book until the special event, to feel as grown-up as their older siblings or parents who might also be members of book groups, and to become part of an engaged core group of children meeting monthly to celebrate reading. Who knows, you might be the person that sets up a child for a lifetime habit of sharing stories with friends or even beginning their own book discussion group.

5

SKILL: DISCOVERING ENGINEERING, ART, AND DESIGN TO INCREASE THE VISUAL LITERACY OF CHILDREN AGED FIVE TO SEVEN

The SKILL program introduces five-to-seven-year-olds to the idea that engineering, art, and design is all around them, from the boxes their favorite cereals are packaged in to the weight and grip of the pencil in their hands. The SKILL program is designed to widen the observational skills of children and encourage their curiosity about the world around them, to help them ask questions of others but never be afraid to explore their own answers.

In the buildings we live and work in and the products we buy, there exists both science and artistry. Though technology is taking us places faster and further than ever before, sometimes a simple cardboard box provides our imaginations the perfect launchpad from which to begin.

As you will see in the three programs outlined below, picture books are the perfect entry to sharpening the techniques of observation. Visual literacy allows readers and listeners—the observers, if you will—the opportunity to bridge the gap between the written text and the combination of the words and illustrations.

FRIENDSHIPS ARE THE (BOW) TIES THAT BIND

Andrew Prahin's *Brimsby's Hats* tells the story of a quintessential Maker: maker of hats, maker of homes, and maker of friendships. This picture book exemplifies how the Maker Movement brings people together, not merely as makers of objects but builders of bonds. It is also an introduction to the world of clothing and accessories and the work involved in transforming a fashion design idea into a tangible product.

Friendships Are the (Bow) Ties That Bind begins with a read-aloud of *Brimsby's Hats*. Next, introduce the participants to Mo Bridges, a 13-year-old bow tie designer and CEO of his own business, Mo's Bows. Allow the children to become their own clothing and accessory designers by exploring the Osmo Masterpiece app and finishing the program with the Maker element, embellishing a paper bag vest.

Children will be entranced by a reading of Brimsby's story, a hat maker whose best friend leaves to follow his dream of becoming a sea captain. Brimsby uses his Maker mindset by sharing his accessory design and construction skills to help others in need, making new friends all the while.

Brimsby's Hats provides a natural transition to learning about Moziah "Mo" Bridges, and of Mo's Bows, a company he started when he was only nine years old. Mo has always preferred to dress stylishly and turned an interest in fashion and bow ties into a family business. Mo finds it important to give back to the community with his charity Go Mo!, which allows kids to enjoy summer camp. Online information and video clips about Mo's Bows abound, and you and your participants will be inspired by Mo and his family.

Clothing designers usually start the design process by transferring the ideas in their heads onto paper, or more recently, to tablet. Drawing their visions helps them plan how best to proceed with their designs and construction and allows them to play with different color choices. One way to simulate this process is with the Osmo Masterpiece app.

Drawing the human form is a very difficult task to master. The Osmo Masterpiece app allows users to take photographs of themselves, freeing them to place all their energy into clothing and accessory design. Having taken a picture of themselves, children draw the generated outline onto a piece of paper and then color in this picture using any color schemes or designs that they would like to wear on their outlined clothing.

App Review: Osmo Masterpiece (iOS)

Osmo Masterpiece allows users to shoot a photograph, choose an image already on the iPad's camera roll, or select a clipart image from the gallery within the app, which the app translates into an outline, like a coloring sheet. Users place a piece of paper in front of the iPad and Osmo Masterpiece guides users in tracing the outline precisely onto the paper, regardless of artistic expertise or aptitude. An adjustable slider sets the outline of the image from a single line like a coloring sheet to a textured drawing similar to a sketch. The most important thing users must keep in mind is that they must watch the screen of the iPad as they draw, not their hands or the drawing implement.

This program's Maker element lets kids put form to their virtual ideas by decorating and embellishing a large paper bag vest. You will need to prepare the paper bags before the program:

- Provide one large paper bag for each participant.
- Cut a circular hole in the bottom of the bag for the child's head.
- Cut holes for each arm from the sides of the bag, close to the bottom.

- Determine which side of the bag is the front and make a straight cut on the front of the bag from the top of the bag to the head hole. This is the opening the child will place his or her arms through; it will become the front of the vest.

- The end result should resemble a sleeveless version of a paper smock worn in a doctor's office.

Place the prepared paper bags and any art and craft supplies you have on hand onto a table. Children may color designs or patterns onto their vests and add fun embellishments, such as pom-poms, sequins, or feathers. Fringe is easy to make by cutting vertical slits in the bag. If time allows, conduct an impromptu fashion show and have the children show off their designs by walking down your program room's "runway."

Look down at what you are wearing right now. Much thought and manpower has gone into your clothing's design, manufacturing, and commerce. Friendships Are the (Bow) Ties That Bind will give children a new appreciation for clothing and prove that, like Brimsby and Mo, they can still be little and have super-size dreams.

TINY HOUSES, BIG DESIGN

Any overview of architecture would naturally include buildings built on the grandest of scales: cathedrals, castles, and the world's tallest skyscrapers. But imagine for a moment the challenges and limitations, yet freedom and possibilities, of designing and building structures of a much smaller size. The tiny house movement, initially scoffed at, is gaining momentum. Along with its benefits for adults, it allows children an accessible entry point into the discovery of the science and art of architecture.

Dreaming Up: A Celebration of Building by Christy Hale introduces children to a selection of the world's most diverse architectural design and building materials and presents a read-aloud that will leave listeners eager to begin construction on their own dwellings. A presentation of the tiny house phenomenon and SCADpads (experimental homes created in parking garages) will hone their thinking for a later Maker element. Refine their design skills with a virtual makeover of your program room and then explore the Little House Decorator app. Finally, children will construct their own tiny houses using cardboard boxes and art supplies.

Each two-page spread in the book *Dreaming Up: A Celebration of Building* presents a photograph of an exemplary piece of architecture on one side and a short poem on the other, accompanied by an illustration of children using everyday household objects and materials to re-create the structure on a smaller scale. More in-depth information on the buildings and their architects may be found at the back of the book. As you read the book aloud to the group, discuss the different materials the buildings are constructed of and how the surrounding environment might have had a hand in their shapes or functions. Consider inter-library loaning a copy of the book for each child to take home upon registration and return on program day. This will allow the children the opportunity to experiment with different building materials at home and/or learn more about the featured structures and architects.

The tiny house movement involves more than just living in a small house. These houses are usually no more than 400 square feet. What can you fit in a tiny house? Not much; so living in one makes us more aware of what we really need to live, decluttering our lives and lessening our impact on the environment. Tiny houses are much, much cheaper than the average home, allowing these home owners to stop working simply to pay off a house, affording greater physical and financial freedom for personal experiences. Some people hook up their tiny houses to a trailer and drive them around the country. Now that's a mobile home! An online search should produce many examples and styles of tiny houses from which to put together a quick presentation.

SCADpads are similar to tiny houses in that they also explore designing and living in small spaces, in this case two parking spaces within a parking garage. As people return to the cities for the employment and cultural experiences they offer, they are beginning to care less about the size of their living quarters, offsetting the smaller space with the advantages of an urban lifestyle. Students and faculty of Atlanta, Georgia's, Savannah College of Art and Design (SCAD) developed the SCADpad, a living space including all the necessary functional areas for cooking, sleeping, and bathrooms within the perimeter of one parking space. Each team was given two parking spaces (one as a living area and one as a courtyard) within a campus parking garage, and students and faculty both built and lived in the SCADpads as part of an experiment. As with the tiny houses, much online material exists on SCADpads, and visual examples and interviews are available.

Speaking of tiny spaces, maybe it would be fun to give your program room a makeover. Most household paint companies offer room visualizers on their websites. These sites allow you to upload a photograph of a room or house and play with different colored paint samples. It was fun to hear which color combinations our participants wanted to see the program area repainted in and watch their reactions when viewing the results. Room visualizers provide a much faster, cheaper way to test color options than painting swatches on a wall, and they allow the children to see that their creative input has an impact on their surroundings.

Now that the children have had time to play with changing the colors of a room, let them experiment with some more interior design with the Little House Decorator app.

App Review: Little House Decorator (iOS)

Part doll house, part sticker book, this easy-to-use interior decoration app provides little ones with a creative outlet to design, dream, and play. To start, users choose from among four houses on a suburban street or a tree house. They then drag, drop, and resize or rotate 100 home goods and characters, including people, animals, furniture, appliances, lamps, art, and more. There are no time limits and no goals. Little decorators are encouraged to enjoy the creative process at their own pace and design whatever type of living interior appeals to them.

Now the children will be more than ready to design and construct their own tiny houses from cardboard boxes and any art supplies you have on hand. We had our cataloging department save boxes from book orders and provided one box for each participant. We also saved cardboard tubes and the children made quick work of them as castle turrets, guard towers, and entrance tunnels. If possible, provide discarded magazines, scissors, and glue; children may cut out pictures of furniture, windows, and landscaping to decorate the interiors and exteriors of their homes. Let their imaginations run wild, and allow the remainder of the time for their constructions. Walk around the room, asking children about their design choices; their innovation and invention will surely inspire you. Depending on the size of the cardboard boxes and the amount of glue holding the embellishments together, parents and caregivers might be called on to offer a helping hand to carry projects home.

Tiny Houses, Big Design reinforces the premise that children are natural builders and makers. The architects highlighted in Christy Hale's *Dreaming Up: A Celebration of Building* discuss how their childhoods shaped their own future careers and successes. Perhaps one day we'll be studying or living in the architecture of one or more of the children in *your* program!

TESTING, TESTING

The list of chores to do around the home seems never ending. Robots are becoming more and more commonplace to take care of some of the worst jobs: window washing, gutter clearing, lawn mowing, and even pool cleaning. Robots are machines designed to be programmed with a set of instructions to perform a particular task. Sensors allow the machines to take in information from the outside, such as temperature and boundaries, and the robot's computer uses this information, along with the preprogrammed instructions, to tell itself how to best perform its job. For example, a robotic vacuum cleans your floors all by itself, turning when it senses walls, furniture, and other obstacles.

Robots work outside of the home too: welding automobile parts in factories; delivering medicine to nursing stations in hospitals; and a robonaut, a robot astronaut, has even flown aboard the International Space Station. Who engineers and builds robots? A roboticist! And like any other scientist, a roboticist uses research, design, trial and error, testing, and continuing research and development to create robots to help humans perform tasks and jobs.

In Testing, Testing, children become both roboticists and robots, testing and retesting scientific processes to see what works best. The program begins with a read-aloud of Mac Barnett's *Oh No! (Or How My Science Project Destroyed the World)* followed by an app exploration of Toca Robot Lab. Participants then play a game of Robot Says and compete in a Man versus Machine Maker element, creating a clay sculpture alongside a 3D printer.

The young female roboticist in Mac Barnett's *Oh No! (Or How My Science Project Destroyed the World)* is proud when she wins first place in her science fair by building a robot. But the flaws in her design are quickly realized when the robot wreaks havoc on the city, leaving chaos in its wake. As the girl attempts to gain control of her robot, she tries to determine what she should have done differently to make the robot work the way she intended. With this reflection and knowledge, she heads back to her lab to make a new robot to help her destroy the original. Though improved, she finds that this new robot could use a little more tweaking. While reading the story aloud, point out the young roboticist's use of the scientific method and discuss how this sort of thinking could be beneficial in solving problems not only in the science lab but in other areas of life.

After the read-aloud, it is time for the children to become roboticists themselves. Children explore the Toca Robot Lab app to practice designing and building robots of their own.

App Review: Toca Robot Lab (iOS)

There is no learning curve for users of Toca Boca's Robot Lab app. Kids will dive right in, choosing to build their robot from one of three templates: sets of legs, bodies, head, and right and then left arms. The materials offered are all scrap items, sending a subtle message about the benefits of recycling. Once the robot is complete, users fly it through the test lab, a small obstacle course, earning the robot's certification. Each session offers users new sets of recycled materials from which to create a seemingly endless variety of robots. Toca Robot Lab is truly as described, a "digital toy."

The roboticists become the robots with a lively game of Robot Says. It is played in the same manner as Simon Says, except as you call out instructions to your little robots, they must listen carefully and only perform the actions if the commands are preceded by "Robot Says." This is a very simple, verbal way of introducing the concept of computer coding.

Now that the children have had the chance to be both the robot and roboticist, it's time for them to think and reflect on the advantages and limitations of robots and humans through the program's Maker element. Introduce your library's 3D printer to the class and explain how it works. Provide a demonstration of a build from start to finish. Before the program, 3D print a variety of small builds and allow each child to choose one. Provide the children with clay and ask them to replicate the design of their chosen 3D printed object as best they can. Leave time at the end of the program to compare the different objects with the children. Discuss the impressions they have of the objects:

- Which object did they like better and why?
- What can they do that the 3D printer can't?
- What can the 3D printer do that they can't?
- Which process would they prefer to try again, creating a 3D printed object or a clay object?

Testing, Testing is an example of a program that shows that a picture book can have real-world applications. It also represents an opportunity to teach children that actions and decisions have consequences. Just as the girl roboticist in Mac Barnett's *Oh No! (Or How My Science Project Destroyed the World)* did, they must learn that they need to think about their desired outcomes and alter their actions accordingly.

The SKILL programs outlined in this chapter merely scratch the surface of a child's awakening to the observations of his or her surroundings. Many adults lament that there is nothing left on this planet to discover or new lands to explore. Children uncover discoveries every day; a backyard can be just as exciting to explore as a new continent. Sharing quality picture books with children and talking about those books will naturally lead to other subjects of interest. Take time to explore new topics that are interesting to you, and allow your discoveries to guide your program planning. Introduce children to new ideas and innovations and we guarantee they will introduce many more to you.

6

ARTERACTIVE BOOKS: A PROGRAM FOR CHILDREN AGED SIX TO SEVEN CENTERED ON AN INTERACTIVE BOOK OR BOOK APP

ARTeractive Books is a technological story time with an emphasis on art for children aged six and seven. This program differs from a traditional story time for younger children in that participants take a more active role in the reading component. You can share the interactive books or book apps together, with everyone reading as you go, while the activities and artistic Maker elements supplement and reinforce the concepts being presented. We conduct these programs using multiple iPads, but you may modify the directions to fit the number of iPads or tablets available.

Because the interactive books or book apps are the focus of the program, you might wish to plan a strategy on how best to share them with a group. If you have multiple iPads or tablets, you might want to employ a little trick we use when sharing interactive books or book apps.

In order to ensure that all the children remain on the same page, we play a game when it's time to advance to the next screen. Giving the verbal prompt "One, two, three . . . go!" in a variety of vocal inflections (soft, loud, silly, sweet) while varying the amount of time you pause between the countdown and the final "go" makes the children stop, take notice of your command, and react in unison. For some reason, the kids treat it as if it were a game, seeing if they can swipe at *just* the right moment. This practice subtly maintains the focus of the group.

Below are three ARTeractive Books themes. Feel free to use them exactly as written, with changes or adaptations, or as a template for your own favorite themes.

ONE PLANET, TWO PLANET, RED PLANET, BLUE PLANET

Young children are fascinated by, and sometimes a little skeptical about, the existence of planets arranged in an orderly universe. After all, adults talking about giant orbs floating around in the sky that, for the most part, they can't see? To a youngster, that might sound a bit farfetched. One Planet, Two Planet, Red Planet, Blue Planet helps to counter that doubt and perhaps even spark an interest in all things astronomical.

This program is built around the interactive book *There's No Place Like Space* by Dr. Seuss because of its familiar characters (The Cat in the Hat, Thing 1, Thing 2) and age-appropriate language and planetary information. However, because the book features only illustrations of planets, we added a YouTube video featuring photographic images of all of the planets. That gives the children reassurance that yes, unlike the Tooth Fairy, planets are real. After a discussion of planetary differences and similarities and a literacy game, the children conduct a group sharing of *There's No Place Like Space* and create and decorate planets-on-a-stick clay sculptures.

To provide the children with the basic framework of the solar system, offer them a collection of realistic photos and/or video of all the planets. An online search should quickly generate a selection of media choices. During the viewing, point out the notable features, size, and colors of each of the orbs. Asking the children if they can find any other differences and similarities will likely elicit more planetary facts. Allow this discussion to segue the program into a literacy game.

MakerStory is a fun literacy game we created. Write the names of each of the planets on an easel or within your planetary presentation. Explain to the children that most words have enough letters to make smaller words from their rearrangement. For example, the word "Saturn" would yield sat, turn, run, tan, and sun, among others. After the participants develop a group of words from all of the planets, assemble a story with the children using these words as an outline and filling in the rest of the story with their imaginations. Your story might or might not "revolve around" a planetary theme, but this activity provides an interesting opportunity to discover what sort of story the children will create using a base set of words.

As a group, share the interactive story *There's No Place Like Space*. In order to keep the children on the same page, use the "One, two, three . . . go!" method from this chapter's introduction.

App Review: There's No Place Like Space (iOS)

Beloved character the Cat in the Hat and his silly set of friends, Thing 1 and Thing 2, join with animated youngsters Dick and Sally in the first Cat in the Hat's Learning Library adventure. Users choose either "read it myself" or "read to me" before they blast off in a rocket on a scientific exploration of the planets. Vocabulary and presentation are geared to be easily understood by the target age range, five to eight. Users touch words or objects to see the words spelled out and hear them spoken. Text boxes with additional facts open with a tap. The text, illustrations, and narration are full of lyrical Seussian charm. There's No Place Like Space strikes the proper balance between fun and learning.

The children have now learned about the planets in a variety of ways: through film, discussion, story generation, and interacting with an ebook. The Maker element allows them to channel that knowledge into an artistic vision to create planets-on-a-stick sculptures using clay, wooden dowels, cardboard, and glitter glue. Though many different art supplies may be used to create such sculptures, we used the following materials in our program:

- One 25-pound slab of air-dry clay to create a sturdy sculpture base
- Fishing line
- Paper plates
- A selection of Crayola Model Magic® in a variety of colors
- Wooden dowels
- Cardboard precut into doughnut-shaped rings
- Glitter glue in an assortment of colors

Assemble all of the materials on an art supply table, allowing the children to pick and choose as they wish. Using the fishing line, slice one large slab of the air-dry clay for each child. For easy transportation, place the clay onto a paper plate for the child to carry back to his or her work area. They will then shape this slab of clay into a solid base for their sculptures. Children form planets in the colors of their choice from the Crayola Model Magic®. The dowels are carefully inserted into the clay bases so that they can stand on their own. Participants press their planets firmly on top of the dowels, reshaping any dents or impressions. They may decorate their clay planets with glitter glue and/or add a decorated cardboard ring.

Creating a multidisciplinary approach to learning about the planets might seem like an alien concept, but it is actually simple, fun, and effective. This approach allows all types of learners to join in on the action, providing an out-of-this-world experience for everyone!

POETRY ON WHEELS

Note: This program involves the use of food and/or edible ingredients. Be sure to check ahead with parents and guardians for any food allergies or dietary restrictions. It is your responsibility to adjust the ingredients offered based on the medical needs of the participants in your program.

It is sometimes difficult to make poetry appealing to children, especially when it can seem like more of a school assignment than something fun. To sweeten the deal, Poetry on Wheels combines a book app, songs, and poems featuring an eclectic assortment of things that go and ice cream!

The My Dad Drives a Roller Coaster Car app by Crab Hill Press and the automobile art and game activities app Pepi Garage introduce the program's theme. To get the children up and moving, playact the motions while singing along to Laurie Berkner's song "Drive My Car." Turn the high beams on poetry with the book *Poem-mobiles* by J. Patrick Lewis and Douglas Florian. Put the cherry on top of this program with a Make Your Own Banana Split party.

Start your engines with a group sharing of the book app My Dad Drives a Roller Coaster Car. Allow the children ample opportunity to find all the interactions on each page. In order to keep the children on the same page, use the "One, two, three . . . go!" method from this chapter's introduction.

App Review: My Dad Drives a Roller Coaster Car (iOS)

My Dad Drives a Roller Coaster Car tells the story of a boy and his transportation-savvy family at the amusement park. The app opens with a choice for users. They may elect the "read to me" or "read on my own" option. Everyone in Hank's family has an amusement park vehicle except for him. He asks to take a turn with Dad's roller coaster car, Mom's carousel horse, and so on, but no one agrees. Grandpa even says he can drive "someday," which Hank notes isn't even an actual day. Close to giving up on his dream, Hank is finally rewarded with a bumper car of his own. Filled with nostalgic illustrations, energetic animations, pleasurable narration, and an enjoyably heavy dose of onomatopoeia, the app makes the perfect complement to any transportation-themed program for the picture-book crowd.

Keep the iPads or tablets handy for the next activity, an exploration of the Pepi Garage app, in which children personalize a car and take it for a ride.

App Review: Pepi Garage (iOS and Android)

Explore the world of custom cars with the Pepi Garage app. Users choose one of four vehicles in the garage, each with a friendly animal driver, and select paint in colors and patterns, stickers, wheels, and vehicular accessories to create their own unique automobiles. When the cars are embellished to perfection, users take their vehicle on a photoshoot either in the Pepi garage or any real-time setting of their choice. The blue landscape photo button places the car on the iPad camera as an overlay and takes a regular point-and-shoot photo. In this way, users may virtually "park" their automobile in their own driveway. Once the photoshoot is done, would-be drivers may tap the green car button, taking their vehicle for a fun-filled ride with obstacles, bridges, and more. The controls are easy to use and require no written instructions. This is a great app for junior Formula One drivers, budding car enthusiasts, and kids who love to color and create.

Join in with the children as you playact Laurie Berkner's "Drive My Car" or any other song featuring things that go. This is a cumulative song with many different hand and foot motions and sound effects. It might be helpful to run through the lyrics and associated sounds and motions with the children before putting all the steps together.

At the song's end, all the children will park their cars, offering the perfect opportunity for a read-aloud of Poem-mobiles, the poetry book featuring wacky futuristic cars of all shapes and sizes. The imaginative rhyming poems, filled with silly puns and creative wordplay, are the perfect examples of the type of poetry that will whet a child's appetite for more. The illustrator, Jeremy Holmes, captures the essence of each poem in his detailed drawings.

Because our favorite *Poem-mobiles* poem was "The Banana Split Car," we decided to end the program with a yummy Maker element: a Make Your Own Banana Split party. Due to the prevalence of nut allergies, we chose not to offer any nut or nut-filled ingredients. We have found it's best to provide vanilla ice cream and a wide selection of toppings. This allows the children to customize their tasty treats.

Poetry on Wheels sells poetry to kids without the need for the tactics of a used car salesperson. After hearing the poems in *Poem-mobiles*, kids will realize that poetry can be fun, lively, and written about any subject. They'll likely be inspired to write poetry about their own favorite things. You've put the children in the driver's seat for poem creation; now, relax and enjoy the ride.

LEGGO MY EGGLOO

From their funny waddle to their natural formal dress, penguins have always been a topic of fascination for children, authors, and filmmakers. These curious creatures have broad appeal, whether presented realistically, as in *March of the Penguins*, or in fictional form like the long-running picture-book series Tacky the Penguin.

This program was inspired by the book app Rounds: Parker Penguin. Because this book app features only illustrations, we added a YouTube video showing entertaining, yet informative, film clips of penguins in their natural habitats. After the clip, discuss what additional facts or experiences the children know or have had with penguins. Conduct a group sharing of the book app Rounds: Parker Penguin. Add a waddling walk to the classic egg-and-spoon race for a rollicking good time. Close the program with plastic "eggloo" igloo paintings.

Begin the program by showing your chosen penguin film clips. You will find a plethora of penguin offerings on YouTube and other online sites. Follow the clips with a discussion among the participants. Invite any of the children to tell the group what they know about penguins or share an experience they've had at an aquarium or on a trip.

Now that the children have a basic, shared knowledge base, they are ready to get the most out of the book app. Read the book app together, as a group, pointing out the interactive features. In order to keep the children on the same page, use the "One, two, three . . . go!" method from this chapter's introduction.

App Review: Rounds: Parker Penguin (iOS)

Rounds books feature an illustrated animal in all the stages of its life, eventually ending its story where it began: creating a circle of life. This second iteration of a Rounds app, and companion app to Rounds: Franklin Frog, spotlights the life cycle of a penguin. Users are greeted with a choice to "read and play" or "read by myself." Having chosen to be read to, little ones are favored with a clear narration by a child with a charming British accent. The written words are highlighted as they are spoken. Interactions are pointed out by a blinking halo and impart additional penguin fun facts matched to Parker's current environment or activities. Daily penguin life and habits are explored, including a tame explanation of penguin mating. The cycle is complete when Parker meets Penelope and they hatch little Percy. Rounds apps are the perfect blend of fiction and nonfiction, animation and text, and Parker Penguin is a fine addition to the series.

After sitting and concentrating on the book app, it's time to get up and move. Invite the children to participate in a special penguin version of the egg-and-spoon race. Explain that after female penguins lay their egg or eggs, depending on the species, they pass the egg back and forth to the male penguin, taking turns caring for the egg. Pair the children and give each child a plastic spoon large enough to hold a plastic egg.

Line the children up against opposing program room walls, with team members split among the two groups. Hand the eggs to the children positioned along one of the walls, now referred to as the "nest." Tell the children to place the eggs atop their spoons. Instruct the children that when the race begins, they are to waddle across the room toward their teammate, taking care not to drop their precious penguin eggs. When they reach their partners, they must carefully pass the egg onto their partner's spoon without dropping it. Their partner must then waddle back across the room to the nest without the egg falling off of the spoon. The "penguin" who reaches the nest first with his or her egg still on the spoon is the winner. Repeat this game, producing as many winners as time or interest allows.

The entire program culminates with the Maker element. The children will each receive a large piece of watercolor or thick art paper, a paintbrush, paper plates for paint palettes, and two plastic eggs (purchase eggs that are made to be filled so that you may open and use each half). Place an assortment of washable tempera paint on your art supply table for the children to choose from. Suggest the children paint a penguin with a paintbrush and create a painted igloo by using the plastic egg halves. Children may dip the open end of the egg half into the paint and stamp it onto the paper in the shape of a semicircle to create an igloo.

Although this program might be a little "eggcentric," it's sure to go "over easy" with your program participants. While they are reading, playing, and creating, the children are also learning about penguins and their environments.

By concluding each ARTeractive Books program with an artistic Maker element, you create a space where children may relax and absorb the factual material presented. What the children learn during the program will manifest in the visual representations they create.

7

KIDZ KODE: INTRODUCING COMPUTER CODING THROUGH STORIES AND STORYTELLING FOR CHILDREN AGED SIX TO EIGHT

Computer coding is a language children should know in order to confidently engage in their futures, both personally and professionally. Learning to code is like an all-access pass into the digital world. Kidz Kode's simple explorations of the various forms of storytelling help mature and build the children's intellectual foundations for more complex processes.

In order to become proficient coders, children must decide what events they want to occur and then choose how to make them happen in the shortest number of steps possible. Coding focuses and clarifies a child's thinking. Coding not only takes place in a computer lab; it reaches across the curriculum. In this chapter, you will learn how to connect coding with language arts, math, and art.

For children aged six to eight, it is important to build a set of basic skills and understandings prior to making the leap to the more complex programs outlined in this chapter. You should plan a few classes to get the children's feet wet before you undertake the programs below. The good news is this can be accomplished fairly simply through group and individual exploration of apps such as The Foos, Daisy the Dinosaur, Move the Turtle, Lightbot, and others. Each of these foundation programs should consist of a guided exploration of two or three apps and time for self-teaching. Just as you can't write a story without knowing the alphabet, you can't code without understanding how computer language combines to form commands.

ONCE UPON A CODE

Anyone who has ever felt alienated from math and science (librarians tend to fall into this category) might have a hard time relating to or seeing the necessity of computer coding.

It is simply something someone *else* does. However, by exploring and moving beyond the basics of coding through storytelling, you can attract and sustain young coders who would not otherwise imagine themselves interested in and/or able to code.

In this class, you will view a story created in the Scratch computer program and review its script or code. Then, children will create, code, and act out a simple story in a game of Human Scratch. Now, having mastered a basic understanding of Scratch, young coders can create their own stories in either the ScratchJr or Tynker apps.

The online version of Scratch might seem very intimidating until you complete its 10-minute tutorial. You will find that after you complete the tutorial, you are able to create a multitude of projects, including a simple sample story to use in the program. Your story will include a setting created by a backdrop, a character called a Sprite, and either an action or sound or both. You should prepare a simple plot beforehand. Create a free account at the Scratch website in order to save your story or project. To prepare for this program, you will also need to download the ScratchJr and Tynker apps onto the required number of iPads or tablets.

Begin your program with a group viewing of your Scratch story. Follow that by opening the Scripts area and showing the children the blocks of code used to create the story. Explain how the blocks lock together like those famous plastic interlocking building blocks, Legos®, to create a seamless code. Explain each block and its corresponding effect on the story.

After the story, explain to the children that they are going to take part in a game of Human Scratch. Human Scratch kinesthetically helps children more fully understand the workings of the Scratch coding process. Kids generally learn best by doing rather than seeing. This activity is a way to allow the children to fully immerse themselves in Scratch coding.

Before the program, create colored-paper versions of all the Scratch commands used in the story. These commands are as close as possible in color and shape to those in the actual Scratch program. Laminate the colored coding blocks so that the children can write on them in washable marker to indicate specifics (e.g., the number of steps to take, the costume to change to, the word to say, etc.).

Ask the children to tape sheets of colored paper to the carpet in the program room. These sheets represent the grid in the Stage area of Scratch. Choose one child to be the Sprite. Using the colored-paper command blocks, have the rest of the children work collaboratively to give the Sprite directions in order to carry out a new story. Be sure to move quickly enough so that each child is given the chance to be a Sprite.

Having now achieved a greater understanding of Scratch coding, it is time to conduct a group exploration of the ScratchJr and/or Tynker apps. Oddly, Tynker is much more like Scratch than ScratchJr; however, ScratchJr has the lovable Scratch Cat, which might attract more users. Following the group exploration, allow time for the children to create their own ScratchJr or Tynker stories.

App Review: Tynker (iOS and Android)

Tynker is an essential coding app for beginner and intermediate coders of all ages. Those just starting out might wish to begin with Codey's Quest. This game is a simple introduction to the drag-and-drop, colored, interlocking-block system Tynker uses to write code. The system looks very much like Scratch, as its developers took inspiration from

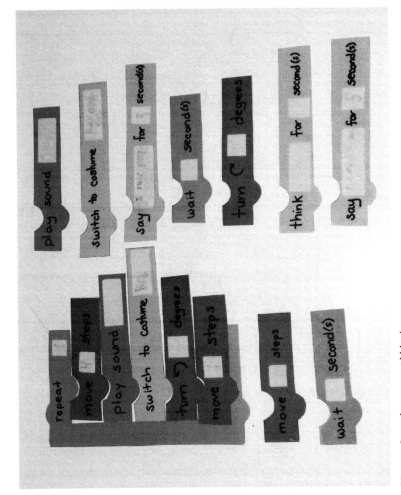

Human Scratch command blocks.

Scratch and other programming languages to create Tynker. Once beginners have completed all the sections of Codey's Quest, mastering a new programming skill in each, they may choose to play different games or move on to the Create area of the app. This area allows users to test out their coding skills by creating their own games, musical projects, and apps. Coders may choose to customize prebuilt games (available in five themes: fantasy, adventure, sci-fi, modern, and spooky) loaded into the app or create their own. Users have the option to work offline if needed. Tynker has also recently added connected device support for the robots Sphero® and Ollie®, the Parrot Rolling Spider Drone®, and the Philips Hue® and Lux® personal lighting systems.

App Review: ScratchJr (iOS and Android)

Created for the youngest of beginning coders, ScratchJr is aimed at users under the age of eight. Those new to the app should watch the wordless tutorial video before opening the app to see how to use ScratchJr's interlocking programming blocks. The programming blocks are all labeled and categorized by pictorial icons, allowing children who have limited reading skills to use the app. Users familiar with the full online version of Scratch will notice the fewer functional capabilities of the app and might have some difficulty with the different interface. However, the young age of the target audience likely precludes familiarity with the online version or the necessity of the additional functional capabilities in Scratch. Young coders will adapt easily to the textless interface and will quickly acquire the skills needed to create their own animated stories and games. Most questions that arise may be answered by the guide accessed through the book-shaped icon on the home page. The lack of sample projects created within the app is a notable negative. However, program facilitators may neutralize this absence by creating their own sample projects for children to explore.

Both Tynker and ScratchJr are wonderful free apps that teach basic coding skills. Downloading both apps will broaden your teaching toolkit. However, should a choice be required, Tynker offers more functionality for a broader range of age and skill levels.

Children who have completed *Once Upon a Code* are well on their way to grasping the fundamentals of the online Scratch program. They can create art, video games, music, and more stories. They will have had a positive experience with coding that might lead them to pursue more advanced opportunities, broadening their choice of hobbies, careers, and more.

GOOD THINGS COME IN SMALL PACKAGES

It is usually easier to learn something new by breaking it down into small pieces. This is true of poetry as well as computer coding, which are the two literacies we've paired together in this program. Though poetry and coding might seem different, you will see that the two processes are quite complementary.

Haiku is a form of poetry that is created in small pieces. For a simple yet thorough explanation of haiku's 17-syllable, 5/7/5 structure, see the author's notes in both *Dogku* by Andrew Clements and *Hi, Koo! A Year of Seasons* by Jon J. Muth, the two picture books used in this program. To be fair to all of the cat lovers who listened to *Dogku*, the group will write a version of "catku" together. The children will then apply their new poetry skills individually to computer coding by creating a 5/7/5 structured animated poem using ScratchJr.

Begin *Good Things Come in Small Packages* with a simple explanation of haiku poetry, followed by a read-aloud of *Hi, Koo! A Year of Seasons* and *Dogku*. In order to reinforce the haiku's structure, clap out the syllable count of each page. For an opposing view, create a "catku," a haiku from a cat's perspective, together as a group. By now, the children should have a working grasp of the 5/7/5 haiku structure.

Having now written the "catku," introduce the children to the cat Sprite in ScratchJr. Show the children an example of a 5/7/5 structured ScratchJr program (for the app review, see the *Once Upon a Code* program in this chapter) by animating your "catku" poem. Begin by having the cat Sprite move five spaces one way, then seven spaces another, and finally five spaces a third way. Next, add in recorded snippets of the "catku" poem you wrote together between the movements, so that the cat moves five spaces and says five syllables, then moves seven spaces and says seven syllables, and finally moves five more spaces and finishes the poem with the last five syllables.

Now it's time to unleash the kids' creativity as they choose a Sprite from the ScratchJr app and create an animated haiku poem of their own. Walk around the room, answering questions and offering pencils and paper to those who need help in visualizing or literally counting out the written syllables of their haiku before recording them. If time permits, share all of the haikus.

By breaking down poetry and computer coding into manageable pieces, children fully engage their brains. It also teaches them a lifelong lesson about how to successfully handle any large obstacle by breaking it into smaller challenges and handling each challenge individually, rather than being overwhelmed by taking them all on at once.

ART: HUMAN VERSUS MACHINE

There are many different kinds of coding; any set of instructions to progress through a task is a type of code. Your favorite cake recipe, directions to the new auto parts store, and a knitting pattern are examples of types of code we are all familiar with but don't identify as such. Even though many of us create art to free ourselves from constraints, the processes of creating art are not unlike writing code. When we create art, we have a mental picture of what we want to make, and our brains send "code" to our hands to achieve the final result.

This program introduces children to abstract art through Barb Rosenstock's *The Noisy Paint Box: The Colors and Sounds of Kandinsky's Abstract Art*, a picture-book biography of one of the pioneers of the abstract art movement, Vasily Kandinsky. After a read-aloud, kids will paint their own abstract masterpieces using traditional supplies: watercolor paints, paintbrushes, and watercolor paper. They will then create another watercolor painting, but this time by sending instructions for a watercolor painting robot to execute their vision. While waiting for their turns with the watercolor painting robot, the little artists will explore the app Morton Subotnick's Pitch Painter.

If you have never heard of a watercolor painting robot, check out the WaterColorBot!®, which was invented by a 12-year-old girl and might be the modern version of Kandinsky's "noisy paint box." There are many different ways to use the WaterColorBot!, but for this program, we downloaded the free software RoboPaint RT onto a laptop and connected the laptop to the WaterColorBot!. The children then drew an abstract painting on the computer, which simultaneously instructed the WaterColorBot! to use its paint and brush to reproduce the design on paper. The process is difficult to describe. The best way to understand how the WaterColorBot! works is to view one of the many videos available online.

You might also wish to create a slideshow of examples of famous abstract artwork to provide the children with additional artistic points of view. Because the WaterColorBot! comes with a simple set of Crayola® watercolor paints, we recommend purchasing one additional set for each participant. This will help the children see that both they and the Water-ColorBot! use the same set of tools.

Begin the program by reading aloud *The Noisy Paint Box: The Colors and Sounds of Kandinsky's Abstract Art*. This story provides a natural transition to the physical act of painting their own watercolors with traditional supplies. Walk around the room asking the children about their art and, as in the book, how their art makes them feel. Allow a set amount of time for the children to paint and clean up.

When the last bowl of water is emptied and the last baby wipe is in the trash, conduct a demonstration of the WaterColorBot!. Next, hand out iPads loaded with Morton Subotnick's Pitch Painter. This musical art app requires minimal instruction; the children should quickly be creating melodious masterpieces.

> ### App Review: Morton Subotnick's Pitch Painter (iOS)
>
> Morton Subotnick's Pitch Painter is an app that combines music and art that you will find yourself using again and again. This go-to app allows children of all ages to paint sounds with the touch of a finger. Users choose one of three instruments that hail from one of four regions of the world. Each instrument makes a different sound and "paints" a different color: red, green, or blue. Children may rearrange the art via the app's tools to change the sound and order of their musical compositions. Morton Subotnick's Pitch Painter provides the opportunity for innovative music and art interplay with a variety of levels of sophistication and complexity.

While the kids are exploring the app, ask two children at a time to come to the laptop and WaterColorBot! station. They may take turns helping each other to instruct, or code, a new masterpiece for the WaterColorBot! to create. Cycle the children through until all have created a machine-made work of art.

Conclude the class with a discussion of the merits of traditionally created art versus technologically created art. Ask the children which they liked better and why. Be sure to validate each child's opinion, because in art, everything is subjective.

Any kind of technology is an investment that you want to get the most out of. If your library is fortunate enough to own a 3D printer, consider creating a two-session program comparing not only the WaterColorBot! to human painting but 3D printing with plastic filament to human sculpting with clay.

Art is such an unexpected take on coding. It allows children to flex different mental muscles than traditional coding. *Art: Human versus Machine* gives participants a more complete mental workout and provides children with another method of expression.

Computer coding makes a game of learning that appeals to this generation of children. It allows young learners to relate to and enjoy the learning of what used to be rote skills. Learning computer coding through storytelling, poetry, math, and art is a lot more interesting and relevant than previous generations' options of logically connecting "if–then" statements to create code. Acquiring the basic skills of computer programming offers children more choices as they grow and mature.

8

NO READING REQUIRED: A BOOKTALK AND TRANSMEDIA PROGRAM ENCOURAGING AND EXCITING RELUCTANT READERS AGED SEVEN TO TEN

For a variety of reasons, not every child is wild about reading. In order to encourage all children to take part in literacy programming at the library, we've developed No Reading Required. This program consists of a booktalk, activities, and a Maker element designed to be so much fun that children forget they are in a literacy program at all. There is no pressure on a child in this type of program. Children don't feel as if they are completing a homework assignment; they arrive relaxed and ready to have a good time.

Even though participants are not required to read a book before the program, it is still a good idea to interlibrary loan enough copies of the booktalk selection for each of the kids to check out and take home at the end of the program. Be aware that not every child is going to take home a copy of the book, and that's okay. It's more important that these children feel like a part of their library and see it as a welcoming and fun place.

For your booktalk selection, choose an appealing and interesting book. Think about the book series, nonfiction topics, movies, and apps that the children ask for the most. These are great starting points for choosing your program theme. First impressions matter; the cover is the first thing the kids see when you hold up the book. Your booktalk should give listeners just enough information to whet their appetites without triggering any spoiler alerts. Highlight the funny, gross, spooky, and awe-inspiring elements. Your choices for activities and Maker elements should reflect the themes of your booktalk title.

Below are three sample No Reading Required program templates targeted at ages seven to ten. You know your audience best; use our suggested books, activities, and Maker elements or simply fill in the templates with your own favorites.

WHAT ICEBERG?

Selected Title: *I Survived the Sinking of the Titanic, 1912* by Lauren Tarshis
Book talk of your selected title

Activity #1: YouTube Videos Featuring the Titanic

Begin by showing children a variety of YouTube videos of the *Titanic*. We chose videos that presented an overview of the *Titanic* disaster, a depiction of the sinking, and a look at the *Titanic* today. You can find the videos we used by conducting an online search by title:

RMS *Titanic* in One Minute—for a fast overview of the history of the *Titanic*
Titanic sinking simulation—original version by clctitanic—an annotated, time-sensitive look at the ship's sinking
Titanic Expedition HD (2010) the Wreck of *Titanic*—Scary Underwater Footage—contemporary footage of the *Titanic* in its underwater resting place

Activity #2: Book/CD-ROM from Explore Titanic by Peter Chrisp

This CD-ROM shows a three-dimensional representation of what the *Titanic* would have looked like from a passenger's point of view as they traveled on foot about the ship. Viewers will be able to look out at the ocean and walk from port to stern, taking in all the sights as they go.

Activity #3: The Science of Icebergs

We wanted children to understand one of the reasons the crew of the *Titanic* did not see the iceberg by highlighting the science behind the adage "the tip of the iceberg." To do just that, we recommend you purchase or borrow a large, clear container, like a fish tank (we bought one at a tag sale).

At least one day before the program, create your iceberg(s):

- Fill balloons with tap water and add a dash of salt.
- Knot the balloons and place them in a freezer.
- On the day of the program, fill the fish tank with cold water.
- Just before the activity, cut the iceberg(s) free from the balloons and submerge them in the water.
- Allow the children time to walk around the container and get a 360-degree view of the iceberg(s).
- Explain the concepts of density and buoyancy and their effect on how icebergs float and appear deceptively small on the surface.

Activity #4: Guided Exploration of the App *Titanic: Her Journey*

App Review: Titanic: Her Journey (iOS)

The History Press, a publisher dedicated to bringing history to the masses, gathered together the research for Titanic: Her Journey from their fleet of *Titanic* authors and created an app that is both academically complete and brilliantly designed. Users open the app to a series of menus that provide access to a detailed account of the history of *Titanic*, including text, photographs, and other media. The app presents an exhaustive investigation, from her humble shipyard beginnings to the fatal night of her sinking and beyond. The depth and breadth of the information provided is astounding. Users follow not only the ship herself but passengers and crew as well. Included in the sea of fascinating facts are detailed deck plans (and everything you could want to know about the *Titanic*'s construction), biographies of passengers and crew, a cool Did You Know? section with unusual facts users are likely not to have known, and an archive full of interesting photographs, audio, and film. Those familiar with *Titanic*'s tragic tale will find much new information to enthusiastically pore over. Even those only slightly interested in the *Titanic* will find themselves enthralled.

Activity #5: Maker Element: Cork Boat Obstacle Race

Perform an online search for instructions to create cork boats or rafts. You may choose a set of simple instructions that include materials you already own or can purchase very inexpensively. We chose to create a cork boat by providing each child with a large wine cork purchased from an online craft store, a toothpick, a piece of paper, and art supplies. Children cut the paper into flag shapes and personalize it with decorations. Poke the toothpick through the paper to create a flag and then poke the other end of the toothpick into the cork to create a boat.

When they are finished, allow the children to set sail on their maiden voyages. The addition of several shaving cream "icebergs" and a stopwatch app create a cork boat obstacle race in your clear container or fish tank. Kids blow their cork boats around the "icebergs" and try to set the winning time.

Activity #6: Faces of the Titanic

Although this program is entertainingly informative, you might want to take the time to honor the survivors and victims of the *Titanic* disaster. Before the program, use the Titanic: Her Journey app to research passengers and crew members. After gathering a list of those onboard the *Titanic* and represented in the app, go online and find enough photos so that you can assign a passenger or crew biography to each child. In the biography, include a photo, the class in which the passenger traveled or the position of the crew member, the amount of money that was paid for their ticket (if applicable), the reason for being onboard the ship, the person's demographic data, and the city of their departure.

Print the dossiers and tape one to the bottom of each child's chair prior to the program. For your final activity, ask the children to use the Titanic: Her Journey app to discover their passenger or crew member's fate. The children will eagerly share their findings with each

Wine cork boats.

other. Even though the tragedy happened more than 100 years ago, this activity human-izes the *Titanic* disaster for the kids in the program. And although they are affected by the individual stories, they will be much more interested than somber.

Direct the children's attention to the copies of *I Survived the Sinking of the Titanic, 1912* available to be checked out.

LUNCH IS THE MOST IMPORTANT MEAL OF THE DAY

Selected Title: *Lunch Lady and the Cyborg Substitute* by Jarrett J. Krosoczka
Book talk of your selected title

Activity #1: TED Talk: Jarrett J. Krosoczka, "Why Lunch Ladies Are Heroes"

Author and illustrator Jarrett J. Krosoczka shares the inspiring story of the creation of the Lunch Lady graphic novel series and draws attention to unsung heroes within our communities. This TED Talk (www.ted.com/talks/jarrett_krosoczka_why_lunch_ladies _are_heroes?language=en) provides an honest look at the creative process, showing how the popular Lunch Lady series was created and its far-reaching effects on the author, read-ers, and the community.

Activity #2: Self-directed Exploration of the Superhero Comic Book Maker App

App Review: Superhero Comic Book Maker (iOS)

Family-friendly superhero apps are hard to find. Superhero Comic Book Maker is free of violence and features friendly monsters and fully clothed characters. Users may cre-ate a narrated superhero cartoon animation in the Comic Maker section or add vocal narration to a coloring sheet in the Coloring section. The app offers a choice of 27 back-ground scenes and more than 170 stickers with sound effects to embellish users' anima-tions. Twenty-eight customizable coloring pages are available to serve as inspiration or for younger children to color as is. If you are looking to create a traditional comic book, this is not your app. Although it provides the requisite superhero characters, users are unable to enter text. This makes the app suitable for reluctant readers and younger children.

Activity #3: Maker Element: Design Your Own Graphic Novel

Before the program, print out a variety of storyboard templates available online. Kids may choose the style of storyboard they prefer and create their own graphic novels, using a variety of drawing tools. If there are children who are unable to think of their own original concept, suggest they expand on the Lunch Lady's adventure or create a graphic novel that tells the story of their favorite book.

Direct the children's attention to the copies of *Lunch Lady and the Cyborg Substitute* available to be checked out.

GET ME OUTTA HERE!

Selected Title: *Ghostly Alcatraz Island* by Stephen Person
Book talk of your selected title

Activity #1: YouTube Videos about Alcatraz

Begin by showing a variety of short videos exploring facets of historical or contemporary Alcatraz. We chose one video that provided a tour of modern-day Alcatraz at night and a second video that provided historical insight from people who spent a part of their childhoods living on Alcatraz Island while the prison was still in operation. You may find the videos we used by conducting an online search by title:

Me at Alcatraz in San Francisco, CA (Spooky Night Tour)—a mostly wordless nighttime tour of the famous prison
Children of Alcatraz available at imdb.com—a two-minute clip from the documentary of the same name

Activity #2: Maker Element: Catapults

Children make simple catapults from balloons and small, round, disposable food storage cups and containers, approximately the size of a custard cup or ramekin, to try and land on The Rock and sneak into Alcatraz at night.
Before the program:

- Cut out the bottoms of your food storage cups.
- Demonstrate for the children the process of cutting off a half inch from the end of a balloon opposite the opening.
- Tie the open end of the balloon closed as you would if you were blowing up a balloon (but don't actually blow it up).
- Insert the cup into the opening of the balloon with the cut part of the cup closest to the knot.
- Keeping the opening intact, stretch the balloon over the rim of the cup.
- Place mini marshmallows into the cup.
- Pull back on the knot to catapult the mini marshmallows.

To create the game, spread a blue plastic tablecloth onto the floor to represent the water. Place a large flat-bottomed bowl, bottom-side up, in the center of the tablecloth. This bowl represents The Rock. Seat children around the perimeter of the tablecloth. After a countdown, the children will release their catapults and launch their marshmallows toward The

Rock. Children who have successfully landed their marshmallows on top of the inverted bowl have broken into Alcatraz. For added entertainment value and atmosphere, turn off the lights and turn on two "searchlights," flashlights held by staff members or children, and repeat the game.

Activity #3: Game: Pin the Prisoner on Angel Island

Alcatraz prisoners dreamed of escaping and making their way to Angel Island and finally to freedom. Create a pin-the-tail-on-the-donkey-like experience with a sheet of blue poster board and cut copies of drawings, photos, or clipart of Alcatraz, Angel Island, a police boat, sharks, and a pictorial representation of a whirlpool. Attach a piece of double-stick tape or circle of clear tape to the back of a laminated cartoon cutout of a prisoner. Blindfolded children are spun around and pointed in the direction of the poster board game. Each child hopes to stick their prisoner to Angel Island.

Activity #4: Exploration of the App Mugshot Booth

App Review: Mugshot Booth (iOS)

People don't usually associate hilarity with an arrest record, but the Mugshot Booth app is an extremely funny take on the infamous mugshot. Users open to a warrant page, where they enter the perpetrator's essentials: name, location, and crime. Next, the miscreants smile for the birdie, while photographers (or the user him or herself rearranging the camera to face forward) easily align the guilty within the silhouette provided, creating their moment in the spotlight—the mugshot. Users may create special effects like bruises, scars, or tattoos to add a touch of reality. The resulting mugshot has a vintage look and would be the perfect complement to any historic or themed event with a sense of humor.

Direct the children's attention to the copies of *Ghostly Alcatraz Island* available to be checked out.

No Reading Required introduces great books, supporting activities, and Maker elements specifically chosen to generate more interest in a book or theme. It's a sneaky way to encourage children to explore their interests or even add a new one. This program also shows reluctant readers that they, too, can enjoy a visit to the library. It offers an opportunity to reach children you might not normally connect with. Every time reluctant readers come into the library and interact with literature in a positive way, it's a win for them and a win for us.

9

GUEST READER DAY: SUPPLEMENTING TRADITIONAL CLASS VISITS WITH TECHNOLOGY

It is an honor to be invited to a local school to promote the library. Guest Reader Day provides an ideal opportunity to reach children who can't or don't ordinarily come to the library. Traditionally, it has been a way to promote books and reading. However, since the role and offerings of the library are changing, librarians need to supplement their conventional Guest Reader Day planning so that children who never or rarely come to the library will look beyond traditional library stereotypes and realize what new things are available in addition to books.

To make life as easy as possible, focus on the most portable technology: the iPad and accompanying apps and accessories. The programs in this chapter feature the Story Patch app, the Osmo kit, or the small robots Sphero or Ollie (feel free to substitute any robot or portable technology you have). Each of these programs add a big wow factor without heavy lifting. The Story Patch app and apps for the Osmo kit are available only for the iPad. The apps associated with Sphero and Ollie are available in both iOS and Android.

The Story Patch program is suitable for use with all ages, regardless of the grade you have been assigned. The Osmo kit with the associated Tangrams app is best suited for lower elementary students. Sphero and Ollie work best with upper elementary children. Once you explore the different technologies, you might find different ways to utilize each of them. However you decide to add a technological pop, keep in mind that a typical Guest Reader Day session is approximately 20 minutes, so you will need to move quickly to make the best use of your time.

CHOOSE YOUR OWN APPVENTURE

The Story Patch app turns Guest Reader Day on its head. Instead of spending the entire time reading to the children, you will spend an equal amount of time listening to the children tell you the story they collectively create.

Choose Your Own APPventure may be tailored to fit the needs of children from kindergarten through grade five. Pair the Story Patch app portion by beginning with a read-aloud of your favorite grade-appropriate book. Follow the read-aloud with a group story writing session using the Story Patch app.

After introducing yourself to the class, explain to the children that today they will both listen to a story and write a story. Read aloud the print book or books you've chosen to highlight during your visit. For younger children, we enjoy sharing Chris Haughton's picture book *Shh! We Have a Plan*. Older kids seem to never tire of the Diary of a Wimpy Kid series. Choose a chapter or two from the latest installment or your favorite Wimpy Kid adventure.

To transition from print books to the iPad and Story Patch app, you might wish to promote and discuss library programs, acquisitions, and new technology.

App Review: Story Patch (iOS)

Story Patch is perfectly suited for quick and easy story creation. Users may choose to create a tale from scratch or use one of the app's themed templates that work like a Mad Lib. Story Patch provides more than 800 graphics organized into 47 different categories, including customizable characters and a selection of backgrounds children may use to illustrate their literary masterpieces. The app also allows users the option to import photos. Completed books may be saved and posted to social media websites. Its simple interface is easy to navigate and provides maximum potential for creativity.

Explain that the books you read aloud all feature a few basic elements: characters, plot, and setting. Depending on the age of the children, either quickly define the terms or ask the children if they can tell you. Then, tell the children it is now their turn. Beginning with the characters, ask the children to choose from the options within the Story Patch app and allow them to determine the direction of the story. After the story is completed, read it aloud to the class.

You never know if you might inspire a child to write a book of his or her own that will someday be read at Guest Reader Day!

THE WONDERFUL WIZARD OF OSMO

The biggest difference in Guest Reader Day for younger audiences is that they leave the experience knowing that they have a friend at the library. While older children might gain the sense that you are welcoming and approachable, younger children will truly believe you are there to help them.

Osmo is an accessory kit for the iPad that you may order online. In the kit, you will receive a red reflector to place over the iPad's camera, a white base to stand the iPad upright, and an assortment of educational manipulatives, physical objects children use to enhance learning. Before using this product, you must download the free Osmo app that best fits your theme. For this program, we chose to use the tangram manipulatives included in the kit and the Tangram for Osmo app to complement our chosen picture-book read-aloud, *Have You Seen My Monster?* by Steve Light.

Once you have established a rapport with the children, read aloud your favorite print books about shapes. *Have You Seen My Monster?* introduces more advanced shapes and features an appealing hide-and-seek element. The children will enjoy shouting out the familiar shapes, showing you that they know them, while adding to their geometric knowledge base.

As in the *Choose Your Own APPventure* program included above, you might wish to promote and discuss library programs, acquisitions, and new technology to transition from print books to the technology portion. This segues naturally into an introduction of the Tangram for Osmo app.

App Review: Tangram for Osmo (iOS)

Based on the classic Chinese puzzle, the free Tangram app asks users to arrange wooden blocks of different shapes and colors (supplied in the Osmo kit) into increasingly difficult patterns. When the app opens, users watch a wordless introductory animation explaining the app and practice with a few simple shapes, arranging their physical blocks in front of the iPad with the reflective device installed onto the camera. Musical and visual clues will let users know when they have correctly arranged their blocks. Once they get the hang of it, users may opt for easy, medium, or hard levels before embarking on their shape-filled exploration. A "harder" level is offered, but Tangram enthusiasts must unlock this level by completing puzzles.

Set up the iPad and Osmo kit on a table. You may either have the children form a line or request volunteers to come up to the Tangram station. The children will see a colored shape on the iPad created by the placement of smaller individual shapes. They must then re-create this shape in front of the iPad with the Tangram manipulatives included in the kit. Correct answers will be rewarded with flashing shapes and happy music.

A math-literacy-centered program such as this is different from what is normally expected from a librarian Guest Reader Day visit. It reinforces the concept that there are all kinds of literacies to be explored at the intersection of picture books and technology. Click your heels and you are there!

NEW BOTS ON THE BLOCK

When you visit a classroom of older children on Guest Reader Day, your focus might change. Instead of highlighting yourself as the face of the library and then talking about what the library offers, upper elementary students will be more interested in what the library has specifically for them.

Because of the length of the books appropriate for children of this age, you will obviously not be able to complete an entire book during your visit. You might wish to read aloud a chapter or two in one book or book talk a series or selection of themed books. Since we used a robot to create a stop-motion film in our program, we chose to read a chapter from James Patterson's *House of Robots*. We used the app-enabled robotic ball Sphero, but you could as easily use Sphero's companion robot Ollie or any other robotic device you have at your disposal.

After a quick hello, present your read-aloud or booktalk selection. If you've chosen to offer a book talk, ask the children to reciprocate with their favorite titles. You might wish to add these kid-approved titles to your collection, readers' advisory repertoire, or find inspiration for new library programming.

Explain to the children that in the next activity you will collectively create a stop motion film in the Stop Motion Studio app starring Sphero, Ollie, or [Insert Your Robot's Name Here]. Suggest that they might wish to have the robot play the character of a new kid in school, as in Patterson's story, or simply allow the children to choose any character. However, remind them that filming will take place in a classroom setting.

App Review: Stop Motion Studio (iOS and Android)

Almost anyone can make a stop motion film using the Stop Motion Studio app. A welcome video greets users to explain the process of creating a stop motion film or animation. A small number of easy-to-use controls guide the process. Future filmmakers point and shoot still photographs that the app strings together to create a film. An overlay and grid help users maintain continuity between shots. Editing takes place within the app using the familiar tools of cut, copy, and paste. Films may be enhanced with music from an iTunes library or users may insert on-the-spot vocal narration. The in-app purchase feature pack adds a variety of extra elements and is worth the price. For the best results, you may wish to purchase tripods to steady those excited hands on the brink of creation. Completed cinematic creations may be posted online to social media websites directly through the app. If the children appear in the films, remember to obtain written permission before posting any videos onto social media websites.

Be aware that you will need two iPads or tablets for this activity. One iPad or tablet will be needed to control the robot, while the other will be used to shoot the pictures that the app uses to create the stop-motion animation. Most children will be able to operate the robot. After taking into consideration the age, maturity, level of listening, and cooperation, decide whether there are children who are capable of shooting clear photographs within the app. If time allows, the children may take turns being robot operator and cameraperson.

Once the film is complete, show it to the kids and let them know you will be posting it on the library's social media websites so that they may show their friends and families. This shows the kids and viewers of the posted film that the library is more than just a physical space; it is a virtual place as well. It also allows you to take a little of Guest Reader Day back to the library with you. It might also encourage dialogue with other schools.

The Maker Movement encourages people to take a more hands-on approach to learning through creation and play. The activities suggested in the three programs included above allow students to take a more active role in Guest Reader Day, thus fulfilling the library's new mission. As libraries continue to adopt the Maker Movement philosophy, Guest Reader Day needs to reflect these changes.

10

THERE WAS A FINE TOWN THAT SWALLOWED A BOOK: A ONE BOOK, ONE TOWN PROGRAM FOR KIDS

One spring, our library was seeking a project or program inviting community involvement. We recalled a recent display of a local artist's illustrations based on the classic tale *There Was an Old Lady Who Swallowed a Fly* in the library's art gallery, a simple slatboard wall located near the Information Desk. When we saw the exhibit, we immediately realized that the illustrations held appeal for a wide range of ages. We wanted to plan a program around the artwork, but we didn't quite know how to best utilize it. A month or so later, one of our young patrons asked why we didn't offer a One Book, One Town program for kids.

There it was! A Fall Family Reading program featuring the work of a local artist serendipitously fulfilled both needs. We created an intergenerational One Book, One Town program for families, featuring Maker programming for all ages. We named the program "There Was a Fine Town That Swallowed a Book" to mimic the title of the exhibit and the classic song the artwork is based on. After much discussion, the artist agreed to self-publish his work as a children's picture book. The library ordered 100 paperback copies, one of which was given to each registered family to keep for the duration of the nine-week program.

We then designed a slate of Maker and traditional programs around the themes and characters of the book. So as not to reinvent the wheel and make it as easy as possible, we included many of the program templates referenced in earlier chapters. We added fresh content related to *There Was an Old Lady Who Swallowed a Fly* to these templates. In addition to using some of our suggestions, you might wish to add fresh content to your library's most popular program templates.

Though we were lucky enough to find a local artist that met our needs, your program need not be that elaborate. If you are interested in the local artist connection, you might solicit submissions from local authors and choose your favorite. Alternatively, you might wish to highlight an author from your town, region, or state. However, if you wish to simplify your preprogram preparation, choose an already published, well-written picture book with wide appeal.

In case you are not familiar with *There Was an Old Lady Who Swallowed a Fly*, the story is a cumulative tale featuring an old lady and a host of animals. As the story progresses, the ravenous old lady continues to swallow a cat, dog, goat, cow, and horse. Our artist did not change the text of the original song but added different visual clues within his illustrations to extend the story. For example, he drew a doctor reading an X-ray of the animals chasing each other inside the old lady.

Although some authors softened the tale by removing all reference to death, our illustrator chose to keep the original verse intact. Initially, we worried that some parents would object to exposing their small children to the concept. We didn't want to just hand them the book without making them aware of this sensitive issue. So, upon registration, we handed each adult a book with a verbal disclaimer that in the tale the old lady dies; however, we suggested that if the child was sensitive, perhaps the old lady could cry instead. The adult was then free to take the book or refuse it, but either way, they were welcome to attend all the related programming.

Due to the fact that there were so many events associated with There Was a Fine Town That Swallowed a Book, we decided to create a double-sided calendar for patrons. The calendar front simply featured dates and titles of each program. The back contained a full description of each program, including age and registration requirements. We designed the calendar to look like a piece of flypaper hanging from a knotted string of raffia so that it could hang on a clip, nail, or door handle.

In keeping with the design of this book, we have chosen to present the programs to you chronologically by target audience age rather than date, with the exception of the kick-off and finale. Following the brief descriptive list below, you will find in-depth information on how you may re-create each of the individual programs:

- Program Kick-Off—a pet parade with pets, pet owners, animal crafts, and snacks
- eTots—an iPad or tablet story time for children aged two to five focusing on specific characters from the book
- Rookie Readers 2.0—a book discussion, technology exploration, and art workshop for kids aged five and six
- SKILL—a STEAM (science, technology, engineering, art, and math) program for five-to-seven-year-olds highlighting the tale's origin as a song
- Yummy!—a child-and-caregiver program focusing on healthy eating for children aged five and up
- Pixels and Pencils—an art program for seven-to-ten-year-olds using traditional and technological materials and techniques
- MakerLab—Maker programs for seven-to-ten-year-olds
- Draw Like a Pro—a children's instructional drawing program presented by the book's artist for aged seven to ten
- Green Screen Film—a green screen film workshop featuring the book's illustrations for children aged eight to ten

- Storywalk®—a guided walk on our town's segment of the Rails to Trails pathway for all ages
- Grand Finale—simultaneous programming for all ages

FALL FAMILY READING KICK-OFF: PET PARADE

Note: This program involves the use of food and/or edible ingredients. Be sure to check ahead with parents and guardians for any food allergies or dietary restrictions. It is your responsibility to adjust the ingredients offered based on the medical needs of the participants in your program.

People are wild about their pets! Pet owners sometimes call themselves pet parents. In designing your Pet Parade program, try to be as inclusive as possible and give people the chance to bring their entire family to the library. This highlights the library as a family destination: a place where everyone can have a good time. In addition, this type of program can attract new families to the library. So as not to exclude any child, welcome stuffed animals to the Pet Parade. Include a parade of pets and owners set to a musical montage of pet-themed hits, book-character-themed snacks, and simple animal crafts for all ages. Each child/pet duo can be awarded a ribbon and unique winning title.

We took advantage of the warm early-fall weather and held our Pet Parade in the library parking lot. We placed traffic cones at both entrances of our parking lot to block through traffic. Library patrons parked at the elementary school next door. However, if you have a green area attached to your library or a nearby park, you might want to consider upgrading your location from the parking lot.

Because families will need time to park and get themselves and their pets ready and transported to the program, it's best not to begin with the main activity, the pet parade. Instead, create tables filled with animal crafts and art supplies. Animal crafts are available in a variety of price ranges. You can either purchase them or create them yourself. For example, we purchased an assortment of animal masks from an online discount craft supplier. There are also many free animal mask templates available to download online. An artistic staff member could hand draw animal mask templates as well.

Choose snacks that are both funny and healthy. The book includes a fly, a goat, and a cow. So, for example, you might create two trays of cheese and crackers. One tray features crackers and goat cheese, while the other offers crackers and regular "cow" cheese. Before the program, print a picture of the cow and the goat from the book. Cut out the photos and tape them to the corresponding trays. Purchase plastic flies and toothpicks, and impale each fly with a toothpick, inserting one into each cheese square. Be sure to have bottles of water on hand—parading is thirsty business! Don't forget the kids' pet pals. They get thirsty too. Set out bowls of water in the shade. Ask a local pet bakery to donate some tasty treats for your four-legged friends.

It's fun for paraders to march to a playlist of animal-themed hits. We included "Who Let the Dogs Out," "What's New Pussycat," and "Rockin' Robin," but feel free to use your favorite story-time songs. After the parade, give each child/pet duo an award. We used faux Olympic medals purchased online and left over from a previous program. You could also use homemade ribbons, printed certificates, or even prizes. As you hand each child/pet duo

Pet Parade snack.

their award, reveal their unique title; for example, awards included Floppiest Ears, Bushiest Tail, Friendliest, and Loudest Bark. Dream up as many of these titles as you can beforehand in case inspiration fails you on the day.

The pet parade is a great way to draw attention to the book and the Fall Family Reading program, which our library hoped would become an annual event. It will also generate excitement for the rest of the events associated with the One Book, One Town program.

eTOTS: eBUGS

Technology is the bzzzzzz-word in the eTots program! eTots is a story time that emphasizes teaching two-to-five-year-olds the five literacy skills: talking, singing, reading, writing, and playing. This program allows children and their caregivers to become comfortable with and learn basic technology skills. The framework for this session of eTots is the same as those programs outlined in the eTots chapter. You will add bug-themed songs, book apps, educational/fun apps, and a bug jar Maker element to your existing eTots structure.

Though technology is the focus of this program, there are many traditional story-time elements as well. It is best to group all the iPad or tablet activities together, handing out the iPads or tablets just before the technology portion and collecting them at the completion of the iPad or tablet component. This keeps distraction to a minimum and allows children to concentrate on and derive benefit from the other activities offered.

The program begins with your favorite opening song. We like to use a song that welcomes each child individually by name. Then, add some bug-themed songs to your most popular story-time songs to create a musical segment. Some bug-themed examples are "Shoo Fly, Don't Bother Me," "I'm Bringing Home a Baby Bumblebee," and "Itsy Bitsy Spider" (we like the version by Go Fish). If you choose "Shoo Fly," simple laminated flyswatters can easily serve as adorable props. The flyswatter props give the children an opportunity to practice their listening skills by swatting along with the song.

If you are fan of fingerplays, you might wish to mix in some between songs. Here are some fingerplays that have crept into our hearts: Bumblebee on My Nose, A Fly Is on My Toe, and We're Going on a Bug Hunt. An online search will provide you with the lyrics to these and many others. Or you might wish to add your favorite story-time element: felt board, draw-and-tell story, puppets, or others.

To prepare and transition into the technology segment of the program, we say the iPad poem we created based on the nursery rhyme "One, Two, Buckle My Shoe":

> 1, 2 Clean my hands
> 3, 4 Sit on the floor
> 5, 6 Tap the app
> 7, 8 Look, listen, and wait
> 9, 10 Swipe the page
> Now it's time to read again!

In the first line, you can clean your hands by wiping them on your clothing. You never know where little hands have been. The second line encourages any of those standing to be seated and ready to receive their iPad or tablet. In the third line, everyone practices tapping in the air so that the children know what we mean when we tell them to tap the app to open it or to tap an interactive element in the app. In the fourth line, you are reminding the children that they need to listen to the story and other instruction. Swipe in the air during the fifth line to demonstrate what you want the children to do when you ask them to swipe a page to turn it. Now the children are seated quietly, listening, and ready to receive their iPads or tablets.

When presenting a book app, read the narration aloud, pointing out the interactive elements. Educational and fun apps require you to begin with simple directions, but then allow the users to explore on their own. Walk around the group ready to answer questions and try to spot people who seem to need more personalized assistance.

The eTots chapter includes reviews of many of our favorite book apps and educational/fun apps to download to your iPads or tablets for the children to enjoy. In this chapter, you will concentrate on recommendations for bug-themed additions. You may opt to use apps you already own or choose from the following.

App Review: Noisy Bugs Sing-Along (iOS and Android)

A dozen dazzlingly drawn insects, accurately represented in detail and size, grace the pages of the book portion of this sing-along app. Each page showcases one insect and presents a fact about its environment. The narrator uses onomatopoeia, which is a creation of a word to imitate a sound, to represent the sound the insect makes. Tapping the insect shows users how the insect makes that sound with its body and produces an actual recorded insect sound. The sing-along portion of the app is informal and self-directed. The Noisy Bug Game included in this app asks users to match sounds, and their accompanying sound-wave patterns, to the corresponding bugs from the book. This game is a bit too difficult for the target audience of the book portion of this app.

App Review: Grandma Loves Bugs (iOS)

Grandma might be gray, but she's still got it going on . . . and she can dance up a storm! This fun-loving grandma has a thing for bugs and wants to share her passion for insects through 10 mini games focusing on letter identification, counting, spelling, color identification, discovering similarities and differences, and fine motor skill practice. In addition to the games, users have the chance to watch short films to learn in detail about insect-related topics (e.g., from bee to honey) and use a magnifying glass to examine bug photos up close. At the completion of each mini game, users are rewarded with a dance or applause from Grandma, fireworks, or other visual and/or auditory surprises to indicate a job well done.

App Review: Brainy Bugs Preschool Games (iOS)

The Parents' Choice Award winner opens with a selection of four areas of concentration: phonics, counting, music, or puzzles. Phonics asks users to drag letters to spell a word sounded out by the narrator. Each correct answer helps a butterfly emerge from its chrysalis. Counting directs users to tap the numbers sequentially in a mysterious dot-to-dot formation to reveal the outdoor-themed object. In Music, a trio of grasshoppers, backed with instrumental accompaniment on autoplay or a cappella when tapped individually, belt out the chorus of a choice of four nursery-rhyme favorites: "Hickory, Dickory, Dock,"

"Hot Cross Buns," "The Farmer in the Dell," and "London Bridge Is Falling Down." Ant tunnel puzzles present maze pieces that must be flipped and turned until one continuous ant tunnel is created. Once connected, the ants go marching one by one . . . of course. Users earn virtual reward stickers along the way in each area of concentration.

App Review: Sago Mini Bug Builder (iOS)

Creativity and make-believe happily converge in this delightful, easy-to-use insect art app. Users choose one of eight fantasy-bug shapes and are offered multiple hues to color in the shape. An egg then appears on the screen, and users must tap the egg to break it open and see their custom-designed bug emerge. Everyone knows that all fashionable bugs must wear a silly hat (well, at least everyone at Sago knows that) and then eat colorful shape-formed snacks. Messy little bugs need the crumbs wiped off their mouths because they get their picture taken. Once the bug photos are preserved for posterity, the game begins anew with another egg. Little imaginations are encouraged to take flight, while hand-eye coordination is improved with this fun, simple app designed to bring out the nurturing little mommy or daddy in every youngster.

App Review: Little Bits Studio (iOS and Android)

Little Bits Studio has a bugtastic suite of bug-themed apps, one more graphically breathtaking than the next. The six apps included in the buggy bundle are **Bugs and Buttons** (iOS and Android), **Bugs and Buttons 2** (iOS and Android), **Bugs and Bubbles** (iOS), **Bugs and Numbers** (iOS), **Bug Mazing—Adventures in Learning** (iOS and Android), and **Bug Art** (iOS and Android). All of the apps, except Bug Art, use mini games to promote fine motor skills and visual learning. The two Bugs and Buttons apps concentrate primarily on counting, sorting, and numbers. Bugs and Bubbles hones in on colors, patterns, sorting, and tracking. Bug Mazing takes users on an adventure that focuses on numbers, letters, colors, and tracing. Bug Art allows children to design and create their own unique bug and then bring it to life, moving it with their finger. The rounds of those that include mini games seem to take longer to complete than most apps targeted at preschoolers. As a package deal, all except Bug Art have a similar feel. You can't go wrong choosing any of these apps, but to find just the right one to purchase, head to YouTube and view one of the many videos available.

App Review: Bugs, Shapes and Robots Face Paint for Toddlers (iOS)

This simple tracing app teaches shapes and prewriting skills with the help of fireflies. Users are asked by an adult narrator to "trace the circle" or one of nine other shapes. Little fingers must begin at the arrow in order to start tracing and collecting a set number of shiny fireflies placed along the path. The fireflies jump into a jar, which keeps a running count of the number inside. At the conclusion of the app, little ones will be encouraged to "set the fireflies free." The fireflies add color and excitement to the task but occasionally obscure the start arrow and might cause users to require adult help. That caveat aside, this app is a fresh and colorful take on an often boring genre: the tracing app. Shapes are the basis for math, reading (letter recognition), and writing. Tracing provides much-needed practice in the development of hand-eye coordination and the beginning of writing skills. By combining these two areas of concentration, this deceptively simple app packs a lot of learning.

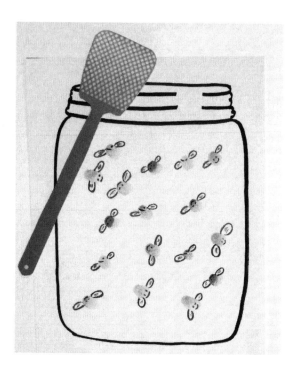

eTots bug jar.

Allow the children to organically transition to the Maker element of the program rather than wrenching the iPad or tablet out of children's hands. Some children will be ready to move to the next activity sooner than others. As the children return the iPads or tablets to you, direct them to the art table you have prepared prior to the program.

The children will create a bug jar, similar to the firefly jar in the Bugs, Shapes and Robots Face Paint for Toddlers app, using washable stamp pads, crayons, and a full-page printout of bug jar clipart. Fingerprints created with the stamp pad will comprise the body of the bugs. The children will use crayons to embellish the body, add wings and legs, and so on. Adults can provide the fingerprints for little ones who don't like messy fingers. Be sure to have lots of baby wipes on hand!

eTots provides an opportunity for caregivers and children to interact and talk with each other while singing, discussing which apps to play, and deciding what elements to add to the bugs in the bug jar project. You can model behavior for the caregivers by engaging in dialogic reading during the book app, asking the children about the apps they choose to play, and encouraging them to talk about their bug jar projects.

ROOKIE READERS 2.0: SAID THE SPIDER TO THE FLY

Take the "s" out of "pest" and you are left with the perfect "pet"—Tedd Arnold's Fly Guy. *There Was an Old Lady Who Swallowed Fly Guy* was the natural choice for Rookie Readers 2.0, a book discussion, technology exploration, and art workshop for beginning readers aged five and six. Mayhem ensues when Buzz's Grandma accidentally swallows Fly Guy in this early-reader adaptation of our fall family reading selection. After reading the story aloud together, you can create a human percussion band with the MaKey MaKey Classic and construct spider string art in an homage to Grandma's second course.

Place interlibrary loans for multiple copies of *There Was an Old Lady Who Swallowed Fly Guy* so that each registered child may borrow his or her own book. Ask participants to read the book by themselves, and/or with a grown-up, before the program. The class begins with a reading and discussion of the story: both the literal text and the visual clues and clever jokes found in Arnold's illustrations. This practice reinforces the idea that authors and illustrators provide multiple ways to "read" a story.

There Was an Old Lady Who Swallowed a Fly was a song before becoming a book, so consider exploring this musical connection. Use a MaKey MaKey Classic to create a human percussion band using just the MaKey MaKey Classic Quick Start Guide (currently found at www.makeymakey.com/howto.php). No, we really mean it. You don't need to add or subtract anything from the tutorial. Use it exactly as it is written. Now you are ready to form your human percussion band.

Because people are conductive and can complete the MaKey MaKey Classic circuit, ask five children at a time (the number of percussion instruments available in the MaKey MaKey Classic Drum Machine in the MaKey MaKey Classic Quick Start Guide) individually to each hold the metal portion of one alligator clip, the other end of which is inserted and clipped into a hole on the front of the MaKey MaKey Classic. A sixth child will need to hold the grounding wire. High fives from the sixth child will create a human percussion band.

After several encore performances, the kids' hands will be warmed up and ready for the next activity: spider string art. A spider was not only one of Grandma's savory snacks but serendipitously tied into the fall and Halloween seasons. String art allows children to practice fine motor skills and hand-eye coordination by threading yarn through holes in precut cardboard squares. This project might serve as an introduction to embroidery and provide ideas for future programs. Though you will need to do a little prep work before the program, kids may jump right into the fun.

Assembling the following materials will make quick work of your prep time. As our library already owned all of these items, this program cost us nothing:

- Corrugated cardboard
- Ruler
- Pencil
- Scissors
- Hole punch
- Yarn
- Clear plastic tape

The corrugated cardboard needs to be thick enough to resist bending but thin enough to allow a hole punch to make a hole. Cut the cardboard into six-inch squares. Instead of using plain brown cardboard, we had an extra blue trifold science fair display board on hand, which provided the string art pieces with a colorful background. After measuring

Spider string art.

and cutting the cardboard into squares, you will then punch five holes along each side of the squares, approximately one inch from the edge.

After the human percussion band, give each child one prepared cardboard square. From a table of different colored and weighted yarns, ask each child to choose one skein. Once they have chosen their yarn, have them bring the skein to you and then repeat the same process for each child:

- Take the cut end of the yarn from the skein and tape it to the back of the cardboard square.
- Cut about three feet of yarn from the skein.
- Wrap a piece of tape around the end of the yarn that is not attached to the cardboard, as in the end of a shoelace, fashioning a "needle."

Children are now ready to begin threading the string up through the holes in the cardboard and back down again, creating their own patterns as they repeat this process. If they finish threading their lengths of yarn, tape the end to the back of the cardboard and allow them to choose a new piece of yarn, creating as many designs and color choices as time permits.

All the components of this program added together show kids that when you close a book, it isn't necessarily "The End." You can create an art project based on a character, connect a song to a book (or write a song for a favorite book), or imagine and write any number of alternate endings, plot paths, and character points of view. Rookie Readers 2.0's *There Was an Old Lady Who Swallowed Fly Guy* might simply be an introduction to fan fiction for new young writers or open up a world of possibilities for every book they read.

SKILL: NAME THAT TUNE

Name That Tune is a perfect example of a SKILL program, exploring the playful side of music through art, engineering, and design by discussing our Fall Family Reading selection's roots as a children's song and the similarities between songs and poems. Children aged five to seven watch a musical performance in Sirena Huang's lively TED Talk "An 11-Year-Old's Magical Violin" and listen to her explain why she prefers the design of the violin over other instruments and how modern-day musicians use 16th-century technology to entertain. The children then assemble and play a banana piano on the MaKey MaKey Classic, explore Morton Subotnick's Pitch Painter app, and make a string instrument from simple materials.

Poems are composed of words, which are constructed of letters, or symbolic representations of sounds. Musical notes are also symbolic representations of sounds, which in combination provide us with chords building to songs. Poems and songs share similar structures and elements. There is usually a beginning, middle, and an end, and they are written in stanzas, verses, or choruses. Both forms may tell a character's story or describe a setting through rhythmic cadences and meters. A melody or tone might evoke suspense, sorrow, or even joy.

You might wish to edit Sirena Huang's TED Talk (located at www.ted.com/talks/sirena _huang_dazzles_on_violin#t-784030) as it includes lengthy portions of violin performance.

After the TED Talk, children will make and play a piano with bananas and a MaKey MaKey Classic using just the MaKey MaKey Classic Quick Start Guide (currently found at www.makeymakey.com/howto.php). You will need to scroll past the MaKey MaKey Classic Drum Machine to the Try Out Software section and choose "piano." Now you are ready to create your banana piano.

Because bananas are conductive and can complete the MaKey MaKey Classic circuit, attach five individual alligator clips to five individual bananas (the number of keys available in the MaKey MaKey Piano in the MaKey MaKey Classic Quick Start Guide). One child at a time may hold the grounding wire and touch the bananas to create music.

App Review: Morton Subotnick's Pitch Painter (iOS)

Morton Subotnick's Pitch Painter is an app that combines music and art that you will find yourself using again and again. This go-to app allows children of all ages to paint sounds with the touch of a finger. Users choose one of three instruments that hail from one of four regions of the world. Each instrument makes a different sound and "paints" a different color: red, green, or blue. Children may rearrange the art via the app's tools to change the sound and order of their musical compositions. Morton Subotnick's Pitch Painter provides the opportunity for innovative music and art interplay with a variety of levels of sophistication and complexity.

After creative play with Morton Subotnick's Pitch Painter, children will learn how easy it is to make a string instrument with everyday materials:

- Heavy-duty paper plates
- Glue
- Markers
- Rubber bands
- Rulers
- Tape

Before the program, glue two heavy-duty paper plates per child together, and allow time for the glue to dry. This increases the stability of their string instruments. The children then use the markers to decorate the plates, which will become the base of the instrument. Stretch three or four rubber bands across the paper plates in the orientation that the children wish to play their instruments. Tape a ruler to the back of the paper plates. This ruler forms the "neck" of the instrument. Now the instruments are ready to play.

Name That Tune reminds us that "literacy" falls across a continuum of disciplines. There are many kinds of literacies with symbolic representation, including music, science, art, math, and, of course, reading, and each has its own unique language and vocabulary. Rather than isolating proficiencies into defined fields of study, we should teach children how the fields overlap and connect. This cross-pollination makes all of the disciplines broader and richer.

YUMMY!

Note: This program involves the use of food and/or edible ingredients. Be sure to check ahead with parents and guardians for any food allergies or dietary restrictions. It is your responsibility to adjust the ingredients offered based on the medical needs of the participants in your program.

The old lady in *There Was an Old Lady Who Swallowed a Fly* doesn't set the best example in healthy food choices, to put it mildly. The *Yummy!* program was designed to help parents show kids that healthy eating can be fun, nutritious, and delicious. Parents and children re-created characters from the book using healthy ingredients. Below you will find photographs and ingredient lists of the samples we made. Make samples from the characters of the book you've chosen, but encourage your parents and children to be creative and come up with their own ideas as well.

Portrait of an Old Lady.

Ingredients:

- Whole wheat bread
- Red peppers
- Carrots
- Cucumbers
- Cheese
- Radicchio

- Baby greens
- Scallions
- Blueberries

Cat Food.

Ingredients:

- Hard-boiled eggs
- Crackers
- Cucumbers
- Scallions
- Red peppers
- Carrots
- Blueberries
- Cheese

Pear-tridge.

Ingredients:

- Pears
- Carrots
- Red peppers
- Blueberries
- Mini marshmallows

Over the Lips.

Ingredients:

- Red apples
- Mini marshmallows
- Vanilla frosting

At times getting children to eat healthy feels like a battle. *Yummy!* teaches children to use their creative and artistic visions to make snacks and meals that are wholesome and appealing. This is one food fight where everyone wins!

PIXELS AND PENCILS: YOU LIGHT UP MY LIFE

Many species of animals have the ability to generate light through biochemical reactions in their bodies, an innate skill called bioluminescence. Fireflies are the most common example of this phenomenon. Creatures use bioluminescence for several reasons: attracting mates and prey, frightening other animals to avoid being eaten, and to create camouflage.

Pixels and Pencils is an art program where children aged seven to ten use both technological and traditional art mediums. *You Light Up My Life* provides children with a science lesson on bioluminescence and an art show put on by Mother Nature. After discussing the process of bioluminescence with the children and watching David Gallo's entertaining and informative TED Talk on bioluminescent marine animals, "Underwater Astonishments" (www.ted.com/talks/david_gallo_shows_underwater_astonishments), participants use the iPad app SpinArtX and traditional art supplies to make glow-in-the-dark paintings.

App Review: SpinArtX (iOS)

SpinArtX allows users to easily generate their own glowing creations. Users choose from 54 individual colors or a rainbow effect to swirl shapes using either dotted or straight lines. In spin mode, swiping the screen accelerates the movement of the design. With a swirl of their fingers in view mode, users can see their object from all angles. The intuitive interface makes for a user-friendly experience. Though the app offers only one activity, if the program is not centered on the app alone, it makes a fine choice.

Glow-in-the-dark painting reinforces the program's bioluminescent theme. Before the program, we gathered all of the materials necessary for the children to create their projects:

- Dark construction paper
- Colored pencils
- Glow-in-the-dark paints
- Small plastic or foam plates to use as paint palettes
- Paintbrushes
- Small cups or bowls filled with water
- Paper towels to blot or dry paintbrushes

Each child draws a picture of their choice onto a piece of dark construction paper using the colored pencils. They paint design accents onto their drawings in glow-in-the-dark colors and allow them to dry. After exposing the pictures to a bright light for several seconds, the paintings glow when the lights are turned off. Many of the children in our library created Halloween decorations for upcoming festivities, while others chose to make gentle-themed wall hangings for younger siblings who were afraid of the dark.

While the children are immersed in their individual creations, walk around the room and talk with the kids about their art. They shouldn't be as self-conscious about sharing their work when you talk with them one on one. Use this time as an opportunity to expand their art vocabulary when you discuss the idea behind their work, how they created their composition, what they like best about the process, and how they plan to complete their paintings.

You Light Up My Life extends the animal theme of *There Was an Old Lady Who Swallowed a Fly* by widening the lens and exposing the endless variety, alien beauty, and strength of the natural world.

MAKERLAB: STUFF IT!

There Was an Old Lady Who Swallowed a Fly is a classic example of a cumulative tale with repeating narrative, one repetition building on the next until the story reaches a climax. The repetition and the rhythm of the cumulative tale, a literary staple since the sixth century, is combined with a study and creation of the *matryoshka*, or Russian nesting doll, in the *Stuff It!* program. Children aged seven to ten learn about what makes a cumulative tale, watch a presentation on a variety of Russian nesting dolls, and use the Story Patch app to help focus their thoughts on characters and create their own cumulative tales. They will then transfer those tales into the designs of their own paper folded nesting doll templates.

MakerLab is a program that allows children to experiment with different aspects of the Maker Movement. In each class, the children "make" something that appeals to both boys and girls. Initially, we worried the creation of a nesting "doll" in the *Stuff It!* program would keep the boys from attending. In designing publicity graphics, we showcased four different sets of matryoshkas: traditional, dinosaurs, robots, and sharks. In the end, our fears were unfounded; more boys signed up for this program than girls.

In addition to *There Was an Old Lady Who Swallowed a Fly*, familiar examples of cumulative tales were on display when the children arrived. A quick review of the examples and elements of the cumulative tale completed, the topic changed to a discussion of a "cumulative" doll of sorts, the Russian matryoshka. A PowerPoint presentation explained the history and the process used to create the wooden nesting dolls.

Once the children understood what a cumulative tale was and could connect it to the process of making a nesting doll, they used the Story Patch app to create a cumulative tale on which to base their nesting dolls.

Because the app portion of the program was intended to take up a small amount of time, the Story Patch app was chosen. This app provides a large selection of stock characters, but it does not allow for artistic drawing within the app. We wanted the children to save the time they would use imagining a unique character by finding one already within the app and use this time to create an original story and draw on the paper nesting doll templates.

App Review: Story Patch (iOS)

Story Patch is perfectly suited for quick and easy story creation. Users may choose to create a tale from scratch or use one of the app's themed templates that work like a Mad Lib. Story Patch provides more than 800 graphics organized into 47 different categories, including customizable characters and a selection of backgrounds children may use to illustrate their literary masterpieces. The app also allows users the option to import photos. Completed books may be saved and posted to social media websites. Its simple interface is easy to navigate and provides maximum potential for creativity.

You can print the nesting dolls from foldable, paper nesting doll templates purchased in file format very inexpensively online. Before the program, remove the preprinted designs from the templates with Photoshop so that only the fold lines remain. This way you can present each child with a clean set of dolls to illustrate any way they want and then fold and adhere into a three-dimensional shape. For a younger or less-skilled audience, you might prefer to offer the children a blank matryoshka coloring sheet that would not require intricate folding and gluing.

Stuff It! adds a new dimension to a popular literary device by combining it with an app and connecting it to a similarly constructed toy or decorative piece: the Russian matryoshka doll. You may use this book-app-matryoshka activity construct with any cumulative tale.

DRAW LIKE A PRO

When we saw the original artwork from *There Was an Old Lady Who Swallowed a Fly*, we knew that not only did we want to use this book as our One Book, One Town title, but we also wanted to feature the artist himself in a program for kids. The most obvious choice was a drawing program. Children aged seven to ten brought a pad of paper and a pencil and our illustrator taught them the basics of creating the forms of the characters from the book.

GREEN SCREEN FILMS: AS SEEN ON TV

If you've watched Superman fly through the air or a meteorologist forecast the weather, you've seen a green screen at work. Actors, newscasters, and other TV and movie on-air personnel stand in front of what looks like a green sheet or wall while the images behind them are added simultaneously through an editing process. *As Seen on TV* lets groups of kids aged eight to ten use the Green Screen app by Do Ink with the art in *There Was an Old Lady Who Swallowed a Fly* to write and record unique TV show parodies.

After a discussion of the green-screen technique, groups brainstorm to choose the type of TV program (e.g., cooking, newscast, nature/animal feature, etc.) they wish to produce. Then they collaboratively write the storyboard and script for their film. Each group member chooses a role for themselves (e.g., camera operator, director, actor, etc.) and . . . ACTION!

Like any TV show, there is a lot of behind-the-scenes work. This is where the staff comes in. Before the program:

- Download the Green Screen app by Do Ink onto the iPads.
- Purchase an inexpensive green screen background from a retailer such as Amazon (homemade green screens might not work).
- Upload textless photo files of the artwork from *There Was an Old Lady Who Swallowed a Fly* to the iPads. (*Note:* The photos we used were sent to us by the author/illustrator who gave us permission to use them in this program.)
- (Optional:) Upload additional copyright-free images from various online sources (e.g., football game, volcano erupting, weather forecast map, food, etc.) to provide more image and plot variety within the films.

- Record a sample green screen film to show to the kids.
- Create a set of written app instructions to provide a reference for the kids to use while they film.
- Prepare a storyboard template (you will find ready-made templates online).
- Gather paper and pencils for writing dialogue.
- Provide one copy of *There Was an Old Lady Who Swallowed a Fly* for each group to refresh their memories.

App Review: Green Screen by Do Ink (iOS)

Green Screen by Do Ink provides a simple format for creating green-screen movies. It is wise to watch the app's video tutorial and any of the many video tutorials found online to get a full overview and more comprehensive step-by-step instructions than are included in the Help section of the app. Though not initially intuitive to all, once you learn the process, it is easy to create a cinematic masterpiece! In addition to photo files, Green Screen permits users to upload video or animations created in other apps. Children use a timeline to merge the film's different elements, combining the child actors' sequences with the chosen corresponding background image(s). The finished films are saved to the iPad camera roll and may be easily shared via email, YouTube, and so on.

As Seen on TV allows children to use their own vision and technology to revamp a classic tale through film, like Tim Burton's reimagining of *Alice in Wonderland*. The program provides them with a positive, educational outlet for their vast media exposure. Green-screen filmmaking encourages exploration of point of view, setting, and plot and provides a way for children who have trouble sitting down and writing a story to participate in the writing experience.

STORYWALK®

A Storywalk®, a trademarked creation by Anne Ferguson, is made by placing the individual pages of a children's picture book at intervals along a designated outdoor route or path. Families out for a walk exercise both their bodies and minds as they stroll along reading the pages.

We wanted to take advantage of this unique way to engage a family of learners. So we created our own Storywalk using the pages of *There Was an Old Lady Who Swallowed a Fly*. (*Note*: The pages we used were sent to us by the author/illustrator who gave us permission to use them in this program. Our book's illustrator was willing to send us separate files for each page.) Because you'll want large versions of each page, use the printer's tile function so that each page is composed of three 11-by-14-inch pieces of paper. Tape the three pieces of paper to a piece of poster board and enclose it in a clear plastic book cover "borrowed" from your cataloging department. On the morning of the Storywalk, hammer wooden garden stakes into the ground at regular intervals along a linear trail. Then duct tape the plastic pages to the wooden stakes.

Participants are free to enjoy the Storywalk at their leisure. They can walk at a slow pace or race to complete their literary journey. Regardless of whether they are tortoises or hares, they will spend a morning reading and exercising together as a family. And that's all that really matters.

SIMULTANEOUS ALL-AGES FINALE

We frequently receive requests from parents to provide an event that offers activities for each of their children, regardless of age, at the same time. The Fall Family Reading Finale was an opportunity for us to give it a try. There was something for everyone: a traditional story time for the youngest participants, a banana tattoo studio for kids aged six and seven, a silent film workshop for eight-to-ten-year-olds, and a dinner for parents.

Traditional Story Time

We decided on an animal-themed story time, featuring the animals in our One Book, One Town story. Below are the elements we used; feel free to borrow from us or use your own favorite books, songs, fingerplays, and activities.

- Song: "Do the Monkey" by the Wiggles
- Book: *There Was an Old Lady Who Swallowed a Fly* with a flannel board
- Tickle: Criss Cross Applesauce
- Draw-and-tell story
- "More Cowbell" by Joanie Leeds (with bells)
- Book: *Peanut* by Linas Alsenas
- Participatory Story Shoutout: *Moo Hoo* by Candace Ryan (with popsicle stick signs for the cow, owl, and kangaroo sound representations—moo, hoo, and roo—for the children to listen for their animal and hold up their stick when prompted)
- Dog paper bag PUP-pet craft

Banana Tattoo Studio

Make the ultimate temporary tattoo—the banana tattoo! Banana tattoos are created naturally as a banana peel browns when pierced. These tattoos are safe, easy, and require only four supplies:

- Bananas—Choose bananas that still have a hint of green. If the bananas are too green or too ripe they will be difficult for the children to work with.
- Paper clips—Paper clips should be either uncoated or very thinly coated. Heavily coated paper clips will not pierce the banana peel.
- A variety of small, precut printed clipart—You might wish to include images of the types of animals from the book. Choose clipart that is either one long, skinny image or provide multiple smaller images so that the children may decide if they wish to make one large tattoo or many smaller tattoos on their bananas.
- Clear tape

The process to create a banana tattoo is as follows:

- Position and tape the preprinted clipart to the banana peel.
- Create a dot-to-dot outline of the clipart by piercing the banana peel with the paper clip along the lines of the image.
- Remove the taped clipart from the peel.
- Continue filling in the outline with as much detail as you wish.

Once the children have practiced with the clipart, they might have time left over to create their own freehand designs. You might also wish to discuss the process of oxidation or the art technique of pointillism. Post banana tattoos on your social media websites to preserve the memory, because brown bananas don't last.

Silent Film

We decided to create a dramatic presentation of *There Was an Old Lady Who Swallowed a Fly*. We thought that such a classic song deserved the classic treatment of the silent film.

For costumes, we used animal masks we had on hand, but you could also make simple paper-plate animal masks. Ask the children to dress in all one color. Since the final film is black and white, it does not matter what color they choose to wear. If, however, you cast the film beforehand, you should give actors more specific instructions (e.g., the cow should dress in white [black paper spots can be taped to the child's clothes], the dog in brown, etc.).

The Silent Film Studio app is a great fit for this program. We highly recommended that you type the text of your book on the title cards in the app before the program begins. Children generally cannot type the text on the title cards quickly enough. If typing in the text takes too long, the group loses its focus. In order to type title cards before the program, you must first insert some decoy footage that you will later easily delete.

App Review: Silent Film Studio (iOS)

Anyone can easily create a fabulous-looking, old-time silent movie with the Silent Film Studio app. The app allows users to create their films from photos on an iPad camera roll or video clips shot within the app or located in the iPad's library. Users customize their movie's theme, title cards, and music. Editing works simply with a straightforward drag and drop. A red curtain appears when users wish to play their film in the app so that each showing of any silent film opens with a flourish. The end result is polished with an authentic nod to the silent film era.

If your library has a projector or a TV with an HDMI port, connect your iPad and show your budding thespians their silent film. The film might be silent, but the children will be loud and proud as they watch themselves on screen. Be sure to post the silent film on social media websites so family and friends can view it and say, "I knew them when . . . " (*Note:* Remember to obtain written permission before posting any videos including images of participants onto social media websites.)

The Feeding and Watering of Parents

As a thank-you to parents and caregivers who faithfully drove their children back and forth to library programming, you might want to cook and serve them a delicious meal while their children attend the various finale activities. If you aren't handy in the kitchen, consider catering or scaling down to serve only hors d'oeuvres or desserts. The parents will appreciate the effort and might meet new library-loving friends. It's also a great opportunity to promote upcoming adult programs and allows you to acknowledge that the parents are more than just "Sophia's dad" and "Ricky's mom."

A One Book, One Town program for all ages was such a simple idea; we were shocked we hadn't thought of it before. Of course, our library already offered a successful One Book, One Town program for adults. This Fall Family Reading program was a natural extension and a win for all involved! The artist had always wished to publish his book but never had the incentive to do so. We were happy to have played a part in fulfilling his dream, benefiting not only him but the families of our town as well. It was as if the whole town got behind his dream and made it happen.

11

MISSION: MAKERSPACE: A SPACE-THEMED LITERACY MAKERSPACE FOR CHILDREN

The rise of MakerSpaces in libraries has taken the country by storm. Libraries throughout the world are recognizing the potential of the Maker Movement to provide their patrons with hands-on learning experiences and unite them with like-minded individuals who share the Maker ethos. The Maker Movement in libraries is merely an extension of the traditional library role, providing free access for all.

The learn-by-doing model is helpful for all ages but works especially well for children. Their minds are more open, and their logic is more flexible. This makes children exceptional candidates to explore the kind of open-ended projects provided in a MakerSpace.

Learning the foundations of the many literacies in a MakerSpace supports and extends the skills acquired at school. Library MakerSpaces also provide a low- or no-pressure environment for kids, as they will not be graded and there are no expectations or evaluations. It is fun, authentic learning that follows each child's natural pace.

A Literacy MakerSpace is an area set aside for children of all ages to tinker, create, and play while building skills from the multiple literacies: reading, science, math, art, technology, and so on. Just as every library is different, so too is every library MakerSpace. Larger libraries might be able to accommodate a designated MakerSpace specifically for children; but small libraries, like ours, do not have room for a dedicated MakerSpace for any age. Most libraries can meet the need for a MakerSpace by creating a temporary version. This could be a cart of Maker projects wheeled out after school, a one-night takeover of the program room, or the designation of one aisle or even small corner as a Maker area.

Mission: MakerSpace is simply one set of themed ideas for a Literacy MakerSpace. You may use it as a template for another theme you feel is more suited to your patron base, as a jumping-off point for another idea, or you may replicate our concept as is. Regardless of which direction you select, it is important for the longevity of the Literacy MakerSpace to swap out activities on a regular basis. As time goes on, you will discover which demographics use it the most: families, little ones, or upper-elementary students. Adapt your offerings accordingly. A Literacy MakerSpace is analogous to traditional collection development; librarians need to be aware of their patron base, what their patrons want and need, and the library's budget and edit the Literacy MakerSpace accordingly. Patrons should see by the offerings that this is *their* MakerSpace.

In this chapter, you will find ideas for an outer-space-themed Literacy MakerSpace. Mission: MakerSpace creates an astronaut training framework through which children and/or families participate in Maker activities. The ideas are presented in geographical order, describing the stations from entry to exit. However, a child should be allowed to explore the area in his or her own way, at his or her own pace. A Literacy MakerSpace is not a puzzle to be solved or a maze to be completed before exiting. Children may explore any or all of the stations for as long as they desire. Older children should feel free to bypass stations and/or activities they feel are too young for them.

The Literacy MakerSpace area should be a place that people are attracted to and curious about. They should feel welcome and encouraged to not only enter but to also touch everything. The first station includes traditional reading literacy activities for the youngest participants. Each successive station features a different literacy competency and/or targets a different age group. The final destination consists of a collaboration station, presenting an open-ended project to which children may cumulatively add.

Be sure to create some kind of signage for your cart, area, or room so that users know they are entering a special place created just for them. You might choose something as small as putting a paper sign with outer-space-themed clipart on your cart or walls or as elaborate as creating a movie announcing the mission of the MakerSpace. If possible, enlist the help of your tweens and teens to film a message from NASA, welcoming the "future astronauts" to their training program. The digital message should let children know that all kinds of people become astronauts and they can too. It should also explain each of the different stations (although not the activities, as these will vary). At the end of the NASA message, "future astronauts" should be encouraged to enjoy the process and make it their own. Display this message on an iPad or tablet, TV, monitor, whiteboard, or smartboard.

The first station is targeted at preschoolers and their families. You might wish to call this station Early Learning Liftoff. It features basic activities to introduce skills from across the different literacies. For example, an alphabet moon base may be created by filling a tub or container with play sand or rice. Plastic or paper laminated letters of the alphabet may be buried in the sand or rice and the future astronauts unearth the letters using small shovels, toy rovers, or diggers. Place space-themed word flashcards with the outlines of the letters used to create words around the table, so that little hands may place the plastic letters within the outlines and spell a word.

If your library has room for more than one station for this age group or this group attends steadily, consider adding more Early Learning Liftoff activities in the different literacies. For art literacy, create a station where children decorate their own astronaut sticker badges. Purchase blank labels and stickers and offer a variety of art supplies for this "make-and-take" activity. Math becomes fun with a numbered "moon rock" countdown. Write numbers on rocks with a permanent marker and have children make a countdown by placing the rocks in order on a homemade number line.

Explore inexpensive planetary science with an orbiting model made from yarn, felt, fabric, craft sticks, tongue depressors, or paint stirrers. Make a doughnut-shaped planet from felt or fabric. Tie one end of the yarn through the hole of the doughnut-shaped planet and the other end of the yarn around one end of the wooden stick. Gripping the wooden stick firmly and rotating in a circular motion, the child will create an orbital path simulating how planets revolve around the sun. Display a planetary fact sheet or books at this station to provide an age-appropriate explanation of planet movement.

If you are looking to add a technology literacy element to the Early Learning Liftoff station, consider using the Osmo kit and the app Words for Osmo.

App Review: Words for Osmo (iOS)

Teach letter recognition, spelling, and build vocabulary with the simple word-guessing game using the letter tiles included in the Osmo® kit and the free Words for Osmo app. Users open the app and choose I Spy, Junior Learning Words, or Custom. They can then opt for Versus (against a friend) or Zen (any number of players). As the game begins, a picture appears on the iPad screen along with the direction "guess this word." A colored circle is filled with the letters comprising the word. One of the circles is blank. It is the user's mission to find the correct letter among the letter tiles and place it in front of the iPad (in the range of the Osmo kit's reflective device mounted on the iPad's camera). Any incorrect guess will be shown at the top of the screen. Users are provided with a generous but limited number of incorrect guesses. Registering online for an Osmo account allows users to upload their own photos and create a list of sight words, spelling words, and so on. This child-appropriate take on Hangman will make learning _un!

If you have enough space in your Early Learning Liftoff station, you might wish to provide a pretend-and-play area with trucks, blocks, plastic tools, and astronaut costumes where future space travelers can build a moon base, drive along the surface of the moon, or don a costume and ride rocket chairs to Mars. Whichever activities you choose, create an "atmosphere" of fun and learning. Providing an area for children to role play and "make" believe helps bolster children's creativity and curiosity, skills necessary to succeed in school and life.

The second station, Astronaut Academy, is geared toward elementary-aged students and their families. Just as there are different types of astronauts (pilots, scientists, mechanics, etc.), there should be a variety of activities for children to experience. For example, future astronauts need to communicate with Mission Control. If the audio signal is down, they might need to hold up cards to pass information to Mission Control. Or they can write and film their acceptance speech for their Astronaut of the Year Award. For a more time-consuming take on the written film, space travelers can create their own "star" adventure in the app TeleStory.

App Review: TeleStory (iOS)

Telestory offers users the chance to write, direct, star in, and film their own TV shows. When the app opens, would-be thespians, directors, and camera operators chose a template upon which to base their stories. The templates include "eye spy," "star adventure," "the band," and "the news." The children then select from a choice of typical scenes for the theme they selected (e.g., in the news theme, children may choose from weather, sports, breaking news, the beat, etc.). Next, users determine which cue card relates to the kind of scene they wish to film. If none of the cards shown work for them, the app allows kids to create their own cue cards. If they aren't laughing yet, they will be when they assume different identities through the use of costumes included in the app. Cartoon costume overlays snap to the face of the star and move as he or she moves. This technology isn't perfect, but users will be having so much fun, they will barely notice. A 3-2-1 countdown initiates the filming. Kids may choose to write, act out, and film as many scenes as they like to complete their TV shows. Shows are saved within the app to My Creations and may be exported to the iPad camera roll for projecting and sharing.

If you are like us, it's possible that you struggle with math. So, for a math literacy activity, we went to NASA, the space experts. At their Math-related Activities website (located at the time of publication at http://spaceplace.nasa.gov/math-activities/en/), there are many excellent ideas for space-themed math literacy projects. Our favorite is entitled "Packing for a L-o-o-o-ng Trip to Mars." This activity involves would-be astronauts choosing and measuring what they will be able to fit and pack in their designated one cubic meter amount of storage space. This is a thought-provoking exercise grounded in real-world applications.

There is an abundance of science literacy activities for this age group. For a simple gravity experiment, demonstrate how a paper clip can defy gravity. Attach a strong magnet to the inside top of a box. Ask your cataloging department to set aside a few boxes for you to use for this experiment, or bring in a shoe box you already have at home. Attach a paper clip to a length of embroidery floss, string, or thread that is at least one inch shorter than the height of the box. Hold the paper clip up to the magnet until you feel the pull of the magnet lifting the paper clip without you needing to hold it. Now, tape the cut end of the embroidery floss, string, or thread to the inside bottom of the box, directly underneath the magnet. Hold the paper clip up to the magnet and then let go to see gravity in action.

If technology activities are popular with your patrons, add a technological element to the Astronaut Academy station. Ask the future astronauts to create lighting for the interior of their rocket ship or space station using Snap Circuits or littleBits. Provide the manuals included in the kits for the children to refer to. You might also wish to present a simple explanation of velocity and lift and provide the Aero! app to practice the science of flight.

App Review: Aero! (iOS)

The Aero! app teaches the basics of flight with the help of an animated albatross. Users must master the delicate balance of thrust, lift, and drag to keep the bird aloft while flying over an ocean setting. The app was designed by Bill Nye the Science Guy and created as an educational tool. Although the app is simple and does not have any cumulative goal or game elements, users will enjoy testing the limits of the albatross's abilities.

The final station is an Open-Ended Collaboration Station for children of all ages and their families. Switch out the activities to provide a variety of hands-on experiences. You might wish to have children create planets and stars or constellations using art supplies you already have on hand. Hang them from your Mission: MakerSpace ceiling, creating a collaboratively produced, simulated night sky. On another week, you can leave out plastic interlocking building blocks with which children may build a space station, rocket launch pad, or whatever else their imaginations can dream up.

For a technological addition to the Open-Ended Collaboration Station, set out Snap Circuits or littleBits. Allow the children to build their own electrical inventions or add to those created by other participants to take into outer space, having the handbooks at the ready for help and guidance. You might also wish to include a moon rover project at the open-ended station. Depending on the supplies your library currently has and the library's budget, you might find a multitude of ways to create "moon rovers." Perform an online search and match your supplies or budget to any vehicle's specifications. Or you can simply leave out supplies such as toilet paper tubes, empty plastic water bottles, straws, plastic wheels, empty spools of thread, or clean wine corks available for purchase from craft stores or online, with which kids can create the moon rover they imagine.

The Sphero and Ollie robots make perfect "moon rovers" just as they are, though Ollie seems the more durable of the two. Have children design a moonscape on the floor using blocks, ramps, and other obstacles over which to drive their robotic "rovers." Sphero and Ollie have their own designated apps. To use one app for both devices and to add a bit of computer programming, try the Sphero Macrolab app or the Tickle app. We prefer the Tickle app as Tickle may be used for a multitude of devices.

App Review: Tickle (iOS)

Tickle presents visually based, Scratch-inspired programming for a multitude of devices, including the Star Wars bot BB8, a large selection of drones, the Dash & Dot robotic duo, Arduino Bean, Philips Hue lighting, and the robots Sphero and Ollie. Users select from a large variety of color-coded action and command blocks that lock together like those famous plastic interlocking building blocks, Legos®, to create a seamless code. When the app opens, users choose their device (users might also opt to use cartoon characters and create a project without a device) and are then shown a screen with a simple command project already created for them. Users may choose to edit that project by dragging and dropping in new blocks or delete it entirely and create their own.

This chapter describes an ideal representation of the use of a dedicated MakerSpace, but every library or even Children's Department has the ability to become a *MakerPlace* simply by offering quality, educational, thoughtful, open-ended projects for children. Learning doesn't require a designated space but happens best in a safe, nurturing environment filled with enriching activities.

*APPEND*IX

Aero! (iOS): The Aero! app teaches the basics of flight with the help of an animated albatross. Users must master the delicate balance of thrust, lift, and drag to keep the bird
aloft while flying over an ocean setting. The app was designed by Bill Nye the Science
Guy and created as an educational tool. Although the app is simple and does not have
any cumulative goal or game elements, users will enjoy testing the limits of the albatross's abilities.

Alphabytes (iOS): Alphabet apps are plentiful, but Alphabytes is a noteworthy example.
The pleasingly familiar alphabet cereal motif combined with the happy children voicing
the narration provides little ones with a delightful backdrop to the learning exercises.
Users are offered the choice of alphabet (actually interactive flashcards), tracing, matching, or spelling activities. The interactive flashcards feature a word beginning with the
chosen letter (e.g., arrow for the letter A) and the activity associated with the word.
Swiping or tapping the photo-quality graphic of an arrow sets it loose. Underneath the
arrow are the words "aim the arrow," letting users know they press, hold, and turn the
bow and arrow in all directions. Tracing provides large, easy-to-use outlines of letters
with inner numbered lines for users to trace over with their fingers. Matching asks children to match words, represented by photo-quality graphics of objects, with the first
letter of the object's name. Spelling gives users the chance to place the cereal letters into
corresponding letter outlines to spell a depicted graphic. This is an alphabet app kids
will "eat up."

Art Set (iOS): Artists of all ages can use this virtual art set, complete with supplies for
painting and drawing with an almost unlimited number of art implements (crayons,
pencils, oil paints, watercolor paints, pastels, etc.) in an almost unlimited number of
ways. Users will be spoiled for choice. Once they select a canvas of different colors and
textures and an implement, creation begins. The app boasts virtual pressure sensitivity,
making implements easy to use and quick to respond. Five blending tools are provided

to customize the look. Users may import photos or images and paint or draw on them. Finished creations may be saved in the iPad's camera roll.

Barnyard Dance (iOS and Android): Barnyard Dance, based on another Boynton print best-seller, is a sure-to-please winner in the Boynton app arsenal. The app opens with a title page bonus that allows the opportunity for users to tap through the seasons as the scenery behind the book's gathered characters changes to reflect the different times of the year. The users then choose to read the story by themselves or "have the big guy read it." This time, "the big guy" is famed bluegrass musician John Stey, who sounds as if he is calling out directions at a square dance. Just like Moo, Baa, La, La, La, this app features realistic page turning and illustrations that have been redrawn and recolored to perfection. Each page highlights a set of Boynton's signature animal friends who bow, twirl, spin, prance, and promenade with each other in what feels like a square dance of pure joy. It'll be hard to stay seated when this app is done. Dance party, anyone?

Brainy Bugs Preschool Games for iPad (iOS): The Parents' Choice Award winner opens with a selection of four areas of concentration: phonics, counting, music, or puzzles. Phonics asks users to drag letters to spell a word sounded out by the narrator. Each correct answer helps a butterfly emerge from its chrysalis. Counting directs users to tap the numbers sequentially in a mysterious dot-to-dot formation to reveal the outdoor-themed object. In Music, a trio of grasshoppers, backed with instrumental accompaniment on autoplay or a cappella when tapped individually, belt out the chorus of a choice of four nursery-rhyme favorites: "Hickory, Dickory, Dock," "Hot Cross Buns," "The Farmer in the Dell," and "London Bridge Is Falling Down." Ant tunnel puzzles present maze pieces that must be flipped and turned until one continuous ant tunnel is created. Once connected, the ants go marching one by one . . . of course. Users earn virtual reward stickers along the way in each area of concentration.

Bugs, Shapes and Robots Face Paint for Toddlers (iOS): This simple tracing app teaches shapes and prewriting skills with the help of fireflies. Users are asked by an adult narrator to "trace the circle" or one of nine other shapes. Little fingers must begin at the arrow in order to start tracing and collecting a set number of shiny fireflies placed along the path. The fireflies jump into a jar, which keeps a running count of the number inside. At the conclusion of the app, little ones will be encouraged to "set the fireflies free." The fireflies add color and excitement to the task but occasionally obscure the start arrow and might cause users to require adult help. That caveat aside, this app is a fresh and colorful take on an often boring genre: the tracing app. Shapes are the basis for math, reading (letter recognition), and writing. Tracing provides much-needed practice in the development of hand-eye coordination and the beginning of writing skills. By combining these two areas of concentration, this deceptively simple app packs a lot of learning.

Build and Play 3D Planes, Trains, and Robots and More also known as **Build and Play 3D** (iOS and Android): A recipient of The Children's Technology Review Editor's Choice Award, this STEM app for little Makers allows users to put together any of 15 machines (UFO, hot air balloon, Jet Ski, airplane, car, cement mixer, motorbike, ship, train, crane, digger, monster truck, firetruck, and, of course, robots) by sliding the pieces into place, like a puzzle. Attempting to place a piece incorrectly will cause the piece to fly away from the machine being created. The machines are fairly complex for this age group but present a good challenge. Once complete, each machine has a different task or activity for the children to enjoy. Youngsters increase spatial awareness and problem-solving skills while learning the principles of cause and effect as they put together their robots and other machines.

Dr. Panda's Daycare (iOS and Android): Little ones care for five adorable baby animals in a daycare setting in this role-playing app that encourages creativity. Users may feed their animal babies in the kitchen, play with them outside or inside, put them down for a nap, and so forth. There are more than 1,000 different interactions from which to choose, and each room in the daycare contains clothes, toys, and more for the daycare attendees to utilize. There is no winning (or losing) and no end point for this app. Users are free to explore to their heart's content.

Dr. Panda's Mailman (iOS and Android): The series of apps carrying the Dr. Panda name are open-ended role-playing apps that provide hours of fun and a variety of experiences for their young users. Dr. Panda's Mailman allows would-be letter carriers to experience a day in the life of their mail delivery person. The day begins in the post office, where users opt for either a package to be filled with a chosen toy or to create and decorate a postcard. After designating one of the 10 animals from the animal recipient board and selecting one of four areas (mountain, village, forest, or fields) in which to deliver their mail, Toto the tortoise weighs the package or postcard and licks a stamp to be placed on top of it. Dr. Panda mounts his scooter and rides off, traversing the various roads, performing scooter tricks, pushing through boxes, and shooing away birds while delivering users' packages to their grateful recipients. Once one delivery is made, the process starts over again with a customized new adventure for Dr. Panda Mailman.

Drawnimal (iOS): This animated alphabet app distinguishes itself from the hordes of others with its creative flair. Children lay an iPad onto a piece of paper larger than the iPad, keep a writing instrument at the ready, and open the app. Choosing a letter of the alphabet brings up an unfinished drawing of an animal whose name begins with that letter. Users are visually instructed to complete the animal by drawing the finishing touches onto the paper. For example, the letter "b" brings up a drawing of a bear. He is missing his ears. Youngsters must draw the ears onto the paper above the iPad so that the bear can hear. Once done, they may tap the green arrow or Play button and be rewarded with an animation. The now eared bear gives a loud growl. Drawnimal provides users with a happy blend of the technological and the traditional.

Easy Bake Treats (iOS): Based on the familiar child's toy the Easy-Bake Oven, this app allows users to bake up (and virtually eat, with the chomp of a finger tap) all kinds of delicious goodies. Users choose the item they wish to cook from a familiar list of treats: cupcakes, cake pops, cakes, cookies, pizza, and pretzels. Sorry, no salads here. Children will enjoy adding the ingredients to the bowl, mixing, rolling out, decorating, and taking part in all of the duties of a pint-sized baker. The amount of detail in the graphics and choices creates a realistic kitchen experience for little ones.

Faces iMake (iOS): Hanoch Piven's right-brain creativity app opens with a video tutorial that presents users with a guide to creating their own Piven-inspired collages. Five additional video lessons are also available to view. Users may begin by choosing a colored face shape and then add objects from different categories, such as candy, music, toys, and food, to fill in the features on their face as demonstrated in the first lesson, or they may start by creating a design all their own. The app comes loaded with a special Faces iMake song that plays continuously in the background. Users may also add songs from iTunes or silence the sound altogether. An inspirational gallery of art created by the Piven family is provided. Designs may be shared via email or placed in the user's camera roll. Faces iMake nurtures the creative instinct in every child and provides a pleasurably satisfying outlet for self-expression that is both stimulating and entertaining.

Fish School HD (iOS): It is very hard to find an app that is the jack-of-all-trades of early learning, but Fish School HD is just that. Many early-preschool apps that target multiple learning disciplines fall flat on their approach to one or more of them. Fish School HD does not. The graphics, music, and ease of use all combine to help children learn letter recognition, colors, shapes, counting, and spotting differences so effortlessly that they have no idea they are actually learning. Duck, Duck, Moose has created an appealing underwater foray into educational skills for the youngest of app enthusiasts. Users take the plunge in "abc," the first of the categories offered, by listening and watching the school of fish form the letters of the alphabet. A bubble in the left-hand corner offers additional choices: numbers, playtime, shapes, the alphabet song, colors, differences, and matching. In numbers, the fish form the numbers 1 through 20, just as they did in the abcs. Next, it's imaginative playtime with fish and other water creatures. Children may tap on the screen, making the fish larger and faster and sending them to swim around their underwater home. Shapes presents a fish formation of six shapes: circle, oval, triangle, rectangle, diamond, and square. The alphabet song features a school of fish continuously transforming from one letter to the next, while a pleasing songstress intones the classic alphabet song. The song will repeat as many times as the user desires. In colors, users choose one fish that is then joined by a horde of fish friends, all in the same color. In differences, users are asked to find the fish that looks unique. Finally, in the matching section, little ones are asked to use their memory and concentration skills to match fish. Applications for Fish School are now being accepted!

Grandma Loves Bugs (iOS): Grandma might be gray, but she's still got it going on . . . and she can dance up a storm! This fun-loving grandma has a thing for bugs and wants to share her passion for insects through 10 mini games focusing on letter identification, counting, spelling, color identification, discovering similarities and differences, and fine motor skill practice. In addition to the games, users have the chance to watch short films to learn in detail about insect-related topics (e.g., from bee to honey) and use a magnifying glass to examine bug photos up close. At the completion of each mini game, users are rewarded with a dance or applause from Grandma, fireworks, or other visual and/or auditory surprises to indicate a job well done.

Grandpa's Workshop (iOS and Android): This fix-it-themed app has seven fun mini games and one unique host. Fresh from his workshop, Grandpa is here to encourage users with a dance or a crowd-pleasing high five. Yes, you actually high five Grandpa's hand on the iPad or tablet. The mini games provide practice with numbers, measuring, colors, simple fractions, tool-related vocabulary, and more. The app is targeted for users aged two to six, but the youngest might need assistance with some of Grandpa's puzzles. Interspersed throughout the app are instructional videos featuring real-life craftspeople using the tools shown in the app. Although this app is a favorite with boys, girls will enjoy spending time in Grandpa's Workshop as well.

Green Screen by Do Ink (iOS): Green Screen by Do Ink provides a simple format for creating green-screen movies. It is wise to watch the app's video tutorial and any of the many video tutorials found online to get a full overview and more comprehensive step-by-step instructions than are included in the Help section of the app. Though not initially intuitive to all, once you learn the process, it is easy to create a cinematic masterpiece! In addition to photo files, Green Screen permits users to upload video or animations created in other apps. Children use a timeline to merge the film's different elements, combining the child actors' sequences with the chosen corresponding background image(s). The finished films are saved to the iPad camera roll and may be easily shared via email, YouTube, and so on.

IMAG-N-O-TRON (iOS): Augmented reality collides with the heartwarming picture book *The Fantastic Flying Books of Mr. Morris Lessmore* to create an awe-inspiring reading experience in the IMAG-N-O-TRON app. Users must have both a hard copy of *The Fantastic Flying Books of Mr. Morris Lessmore* and the IMAG-N-O-TRON app. When the app opens, users choose to "play" and then hold the iPad steadily over each page. The app will read the text of the page to the user and, at the same time, the static illustrations on the pages will come to life. Users will receive a clue when it is time to "look up." That's when the real fun begins. Animations and illustrations from the book and sound effects are projected onto the walls and objects in the very room users are in. In this case, the cliché is true; the book *The Fantastic Flying Books of Mr. Morris Lessmore* literally comes to life with the addition of the IMAG-N-O-TRON app.

Lazoo Art Box (iOS): Lazoo, via PBS KIDS, has combined some of their earlier creative art apps and placed them all in one giant art box to fuel any child's imagination and bring out his or her artistic side. Users may choose from any of four art experiences: Let's Squiggle, Let's Color, Let's Draw, or Blank Page. Each section opens with the same quick tutorial. Next, children are given an art prompt, a predrawn picture with something missing that they must complete and written instructions that are highlighted as they are read. A toolbox at the bottom of the screen contains traditional art tools, and some nontraditional ones too (ketchup, anyone?). There are also stickers to add and some ready-made shapes (hearts, snowflakes, pieces of candy, etc.) that may be drawn in lines onto any artistic masterpiece. In Let's Squiggle, youngsters practice prewriting skills by adding squiggles to drawings (e.g., wool to a sheep, smoke to the base of a rocket ship, etc.). They are then directed to press Play and see their drawing come to life. In Let's Color, users practice hand-eye coordination by coloring in simple objects. In Let's Draw, little ones can challenge their imaginations and provide unexpected responses to prompts (e.g., decide what comes out of an elephant's trunk or what hairstyle cartoon friends will be given). In Blank Page, kids are given free rein to express themselves artistically in whatever ways they choose. This engaging, must-have art app gives children a chance to use their imaginations while practicing their prewriting skills and improving their hand-eye coordination. It's an imaginative win-win for preschool artists.

Little Bits Studio (iOS and Android): Little Bits Studio has a bugtastic suite of bug-themed apps, one more graphically breathtaking than the next. The six apps included in the buggy bundle are **Bugs and Buttons** (iOS and Android), **Bugs and Buttons 2** (iOS and Android), **Bugs and Bubbles** (iOS), **Bugs and Numbers** (iOS), **Bug Mazing—Adventures in Learning** (iOS and Android), and **Bug Art** (iOS and Android). All of the apps, except Bug Art, use mini games to promote fine motor skills and visual learning. The two Bugs and Buttons apps concentrate primarily on counting, sorting, and numbers. Bugs and Bubbles hones in on colors, patterns, sorting, and tracking. Bug Mazing takes users on an adventure that focuses on numbers, letters, colors, and tracing. Bug Art allows children to design and create their own unique bug and then bring it to life, moving it with their finger. The rounds of those that include mini games seem to take longer to complete than most apps targeted at preschoolers. As a package deal, all except Bug Art have a similar feel. You can't go wrong choosing any of these apps, but to find just the right one to purchase, head to YouTube and view one of the many videos available.

Little Fox Music Box (iOS and Android): Imagine if Richard Scarry made an app featuring classic kids' songs—that's the best way to visualize Little Fox Music Box. The three featured songs, "London Bridge," "Evening Song," and "Old MacDonald Had a Farm," are sung by children and play in the background while users see a scene filled to the brim with interactive elements set in a milieu related to the song. The song lyrics appear at the top of each scene. Of the three, "Evening Song" has the fewest interactive features but uses on-screen designations to point out interactivity. However, because almost all of the elements in "London Bridge" and "Old MacDonald" are interactive, users might not need the tutorial accompanying "Evening Song." A music room is provided where users may make their own tunes using adorable animal and object graphics that play notes or short musical sequences, and a karaoke space allows children to record their own voice set to the songs. For the most bang for your buck, feature "London Bridge" and then allot time for users to explore the other songs at their leisure.

Little House Decorator (iOS): Part doll house, part sticker book, this easy-to-use interior decoration app provides little ones with a creative outlet to design, dream, and play. To start, users choose from among four houses on a suburban street or a tree house. They then drag, drop, and resize or rotate 100 home goods and characters, including people, animals, furniture, appliances, lamps, art, and more. There are no time limits and no goals. Little decorators are encouraged to enjoy the creative process at their own pace and design whatever type of living interior appeals to them.

Moo, Baa, La, La, La (iOS and Android): A Children's Technology Review Editor's Choice and Parents' Choice Recommended Pick, the app version of the best-selling book *Moo, Baa, La, La, La* (more than 5 million copies of the print version of the book have been sold) is a crowd-pleasing favorite. Users may choose to read the story by themselves or "have the big guy read it." The app version has the feel of a print book, with realistic page-turning action. The warm and quirky animals featured in the illustrations of the book have been redrawn and recolored to perfection. The words are highlighted as they are read by "the big guy" (the big guy is actually Ms. Boynton's son Keith, who is a very talented narrator). Each animal depicted makes a sound when tapped, and the additional clever interactions add to the unique presentation. From the four spinning pigs on the title page, to the trademark singing-pig trio, to the duck that says "baa" on the final page, children will laugh, learn, and enjoy reading this app, which is truly deserving of the name "interactive book." The only complaint you'll hear is when the book ends, but the conveniently located Start Over button on the final page should take care of that.

Morton Subotnick's Pitch Painter (iOS): Morton Subotnick's Pitch Painter is an app that combines music and art that you will find yourself using again and again. This go-to app allows children of all ages to paint sounds with the touch of a finger. Users choose one of three instruments that hail from one of four regions of the world. Each instrument makes a different sound and "paints" a different color: red, green, or blue. Children may rearrange the art via the app's tools to change the sound and order of their musical compositions. Morton Subotnick's Pitch Painter provides the opportunity for innovative music and art interplay with a variety of levels of sophistication and complexity.

Mr. Frog the Neighbor's Dog (iOS): Tickle your funny bone with this rhyming story designed to elicit laughter. Children will meet a "dog" who isn't really a dog; he's a green frog. Users may choose to have the story read to them or read it themselves. Each page of the story has an interactive element, including a simple animation, coloring, a puzzle, hide-and-seek, and more. Although multiple interactions are presented, each one adds to the story, further engaging the young reader. The hilarious tale ends with the promise of a sequel from one of Mr. Frog's similarly silly friends.

Mugshot Booth (iOS): People don't usually associate hilarity with an arrest record, but the Mugshot Booth app is an extremely funny take on the infamous mugshot. Users open to a warrant page, where they enter the perpetrator's essentials: name, location, and crime. Next, the miscreants smile for the birdie, while photographers (or the user him or herself rearranging the camera to face forward) easily align the guilty within the silhouette provided, creating their moment in the spotlight—the mugshot. Users may create special effects like bruises, scars, or tattoos to add a touch of reality. The resulting mugshot has a vintage look and would be the perfect complement to any historic or themed event with a sense of humor.

My Dad Drives a Roller Coaster Car (iOS): My Dad Drives a Roller Coaster Car tells the story of a boy and his transportation-savvy family at the amusement park. The app opens with a choice for users. They may elect the "read to me" or "read on my own" option. Everyone in Hank's family has an amusement park vehicle except for him. He asks to take a turn with Dad's roller coaster car, Mom's carousel horse, and so on, but no one agrees. Grandpa even says he can drive "someday," which Hank notes isn't even an actual day. Close to giving up on his dream, Hank is finally rewarded with a bumper car of his own. Filled with nostalgic illustrations, energetic animations, pleasurable narration, and an enjoyably heavy dose of onomatopoeia, the app makes the perfect complement to any transportation-themed program for the picture-book crowd.

Noisy Bugs Sing-Along (iOS and Android): A dozen dazzlingly drawn insects, accurately represented in detail and size, grace the pages of the book portion of this sing-along app. Each page showcases one insect and presents a fact about its environment. The narrator uses onomatopoeia, which is a creation of a word to imitate a sound, to represent the sound the insect makes. Tapping the insect shows users how the insect makes that sound with its body and produces an actual recorded insect sound. The sing-along portion of the app is informal and self-directed. The Noisy Bug Game included in this app asks users to match sounds, and their accompanying sound-wave patterns, to the corresponding bugs from the book. This game is a bit too difficult for the target audience of the book portion of this app.

Osmo Masterpiece (iOS): Osmo Masterpiece allows users to shoot a photograph, choose an image already on the iPad's camera roll, or select a clipart image from the gallery within the app, which the app translates into an outline, like a coloring sheet. Users place a piece of paper in front of the iPad and Osmo Masterpiece guides users in tracing the outline precisely onto the paper, regardless of artistic expertise or aptitude. An adjustable slider sets the outline of the image from a single line like a coloring sheet to a textured drawing similar to a sketch. The most important thing users must keep in mind is that they must watch the screen of the iPad as they draw, not their hands or the drawing implement.

Paint for Cats (iOS): Fulfill your feline fantasy in this simplistic art app designed for cats but also just right for kids. Users create painted "mousterpieces" (get it?) by batting a mouse with their paws or hands. When the app opens, humans swipe to choose a color palette. Once a palette is selected, a mouse scurries onto the screen. Each time a cat or child taps the mouse, a blob of randomly selected virtual paint from within the palette appears on the screen and a mouse squeaks. The more times the mouse is tapped, the more blobs of paint are added to the artistic creation. Final "mousterpieces" may be shared on Facebook or emailed to friends and family.

Pepi Doctor (iOS and Android): This app helps take the fear out of a trip to the doctor or dentist by giving children the chance to become little healers and discover what doctors and dentists do. Three ethnically diverse child characters appear for users to treat as their patients. Then, the user will select a pictorial representation of which medical problem they wish to treat: ear infection, cuts, broken bones, dental issues, or a fever. Next, the little doctor is shown his or her patient and presented with a doctor's bag that contains a series of appropriate medical tools, appearing in the order of their use. After each tool is used, the smiling, grateful patient thanks his or her doctor. Once the entire treatment is completed, the little doctor is honored with a round of applause and cheers. This role-playing app might be just the ticket to stress-free doctor visits and, who knows, the app could stimulate an interest in a future career in medicine.

Pepi Garage (iOS and Android): Explore the world of custom cars with the Pepi Garage app. Users choose one of four vehicles in the garage, each with a friendly animal driver, and select paint in colors and patterns, stickers, wheels, and vehicular accessories to create their own unique automobiles. When the cars are embellished to perfection, users take their vehicle on a photoshoot either in the Pepi garage or any real-time setting of their choice. The blue landscape photo button places the car on the iPad camera as an overlay and takes a regular point-and-shoot photo. In this way, users may virtually "park" their automobile in their own driveway. Once the photoshoot is done, would-be drivers may tap the green car button, taking their vehicle for a fun-filled ride with obstacles, bridges, and more. The controls are easy to use and require no written instructions. This is a great app for junior Formula One drivers, budding car enthusiasts, and kids who love to color and create.

Pete's Robot (iOS): You know the old adage: a watched mailbox never receives any mail. This is especially true when you are a blue-haired, stick-figured boy waiting and waiting and waiting, with your trusty dog sidekick, Spot, for Spike the mailmonkey to deliver the robot you ordered online. Users will love Pete, Spot, and their inept but well-meaning robot, Z-123. It seems that when Pete was putting together his robot, he forgot the heartdrive. Without a heartdrive, the robot unwittingly finds himself in quite the pickle. He can't seem to do anything right, but—and it's a big but—he sure can dance! What might be the single best page ever in an interactive book app presents Z-123's participation in a dance-off. Move over, Travolta! After a series of mishaps, the missing heartdrive is discovered and installed and Z-123 is able to save Tony the cat. The robot is a hero, and he and his quirky friends Pete and Spot end the story looking forward to more adventures. Users will be left wanting further adventures as well. Dance on, Z-123!

Rounds: Franklin Frog (iOS): The first entry in the Rounds series, and a Children's Technology Review Editor's Choice winner, Franklin Frog is an excellent example of a nonfiction app for little ones. Rounds books feature an illustrated animal and all the stages of its life, eventually ending its story where it began: creating a circle of life. This iteration of a Rounds app spotlights the life cycle of a frog. Users are greeted with a choice to "read and play" or "read by myself." Having chosen to be read to, little ones are favored with a clear narration by a child with a charming British accent. The written words are highlighted as they are spoken. Interactions are pointed out by a blinking halo and impart additional frog fun facts matched to Franklin's current environment or activities. Franklin's tongue, so sticky and so long, reminiscent of the printed book *The Icky Sticky Frog* by Dawn Bentley, is bound to be a favorite as users unfurl the frog's tongue to help him eat. Even frog mating is addressed, although in an age-appropriate manner. Soon, Franklin's mate, Felicity, lays eggs and a new generation is born, completing the circle of life. Hakuna matata!

Rounds: Parker Penguin (iOS): Rounds books feature an illustrated animal in all the stages of its life, eventually ending its story where it began: creating a circle of life. This second iteration of a Rounds app, and companion app to Rounds: Franklin Frog, spotlights the life cycle of a penguin. Users are greeted with a choice to "read and play" or "read by myself." Having chosen to be read to, little ones are favored with a clear narration by a child with a charming British accent. The written words are highlighted as they are spoken. Interactions are pointed out by a blinking halo and impart additional penguin fun facts matched to Parker's current environment or activities. Daily penguin life and habits are explored, including a tame explanation of penguin mating. The cycle is complete when Parker meets Penelope and they hatch little Percy. Rounds apps are the perfect blend of fiction and nonfiction, animation and text, and Parker Penguin is a fine addition to the series.

Sago Mini Bug Builder (iOS): Creativity and make-believe happily converge in this delightful, easy-to-use insect art app. Users choose one of eight fantasy-bug shapes and are offered multiple hues to color in the shape. An egg then appears on the screen, and users must tap the egg to break it open and see their custom-designed bug emerge. Everyone knows that all fashionable bugs must wear a silly hat (well, at least everyone at Sago knows that) and then eat colorful shape-formed snacks. Messy little bugs need the crumbs wiped off their mouths because they get their picture taken. Once the bug photos are preserved for posterity, the game begins anew with another egg. Little imaginations are encouraged to take flight, while hand-eye coordination is improved with this fun, simple app designed to bring out the nurturing little mommy or daddy in every youngster.

ScratchJr (iOS and Android): Created for the youngest of beginning coders, ScratchJr is aimed at users under the age of eight. Those new to the app should watch the wordless tutorial video before opening the app to see how to use ScratchJr's interlocking programming blocks. The programming blocks are all labeled and categorized by pictorial icons, allowing children who have limited reading skills to use the app. Users familiar with the full online version of Scratch will notice the fewer functional capabilities of the app and might have some difficulty with the different interface. However, the young age of the target audience likely precludes familiarity with the online version or the necessity of the additional functional capabilities in Scratch. Young coders will adapt easily to the textless interface and will quickly acquire the skills needed to create their own animated stories and games. Most questions that arise may be answered by the guide accessed through the book-shaped icon on the home page. The lack of sample projects created within the app is a notable negative. However, program facilitators may neutralize this absence by creating their own sample projects for children to explore.

Silent Film Studio (iOS): Anyone can easily create a fabulous-looking, old-time silent movie with the Silent Film Studio app. The app allows users to create their films from photos on an iPad camera roll or video clips shot within the app or located in the iPad's library. Users customize their movie's theme, title cards, and music. Editing works simply with a straightforward drag and drop. A red curtain appears when users wish to play their film in the app so that each showing of any silent film opens with a flourish. The end result is polished with an authentic nod to the silent film era.

SpinArtX (iOS): SpinArtX allows users to easily generate their own glowing creations. Users choose from 54 individual colors or a rainbow effect to swirl shapes using either dotted or straight lines. In spin mode, swiping the screen accelerates the movement of the design. With a swirl of their fingers in view mode, users can see their object from all angles. The intuitive interface makes for a user-friendly experience. Though the app offers only one activity, if the program is not centered on the app alone, it makes a fine choice.

Starring Me in Old MacDonald (iOS): Users will be hard-pressed not to smile, laugh, and cheer as they see themselves interact down on the farm in this customized sing-along presentation of "Old MacDonald Had a Farm." As the app opens, users create their farmer by choosing a photo in their photo library or by taking a photo of anyone or anything they'd like—a stuffed animal, doll, or grown-up—and effortlessly centering it within the head silhouette provided. Next, users may customize their farmer by changing his or her hat, hairstyle, and hair color. Once the farmer is coiffed, he or she is ready to head out to the first of eight interactive musical farm scenes, each corresponding to a verse in the song. Users will see themselves or their "friends" swing on a swing, feed the ducks, play in a mud puddle, play peek-a-boo in the barn, jump on a trampoline at a picnic, drive a truck, visit some hens and, finally, shhh . . . everyone on the farm goes to sleep. Inside the Parents section, the app developers have created a Play and Learn section to help adults get the most out of the app, pointing out all the interactive opportunities for little users. Children will delight as they see themselves or their "friends" count, sort, sing, and move to the rhythm. This personalized app is a surefire hit!

Stop Motion Studio (iOS and Android): Almost anyone can make a stop motion film using the Stop Motion Studio app. A welcome video greets users to explain the process of creating a stop motion film or animation. A small number of easy-to-use controls guide the process. Future filmmakers point and shoot still photographs that the app strings together to create a film. An overlay and grid help users maintain continuity between shots. Editing takes place within the app using the familiar tools of cut, copy, and paste. Films may be enhanced with music from an iTunes library or users may insert on-the-spot vocal narration. The in-app purchase feature pack adds a variety of extra elements and is worth the price. For the best results, you may wish to purchase tripods to steady those excited hands on the brink of creation. Completed cinematic creations may be posted online to social media websites directly through the app. If the children appear in the films, remember to obtain written permission before posting any videos onto social media websites.

Story Patch (iOS): Story Patch is perfectly suited for quick and easy story creation. Users may choose to create a tale from scratch or use one of the app's themed templates that work like a Mad Lib. Story Patch provides more than 800 graphics organized into 47 different categories, including customizable characters and a selection of backgrounds children may use to illustrate their literary masterpieces. The app also allows users the option to import photos. Completed books may be saved and posted to social media websites. Its simple interface is easy to navigate and provides maximum potential for creativity.

Superhero Comic Book Maker (iOS): Family-friendly superhero apps are hard to find. Superhero Comic Book Maker is free of violence and features friendly monsters and fully clothed characters. Users may create a narrated superhero cartoon animation in the Comic Maker section or add vocal narration to a coloring sheet in the Coloring section. The app offers a choice of 27 background scenes and more than 170 stickers with sound effects to embellish users' animations. Twenty-eight customizable coloring pages are available to serve as inspiration or for younger children to color as is. If you are looking to create a traditional comic book, this is not your app. Although it provides the requisite superhero characters, users are unable to enter text. This makes the app suitable for reluctant readers and younger children.

Tangram for Osmo (iOS): Based on the classic Chinese puzzle, the free Tangram app asks users to arrange wooden blocks of different shapes and colors (supplied in the Osmo kit) into increasingly difficult patterns. When the app opens, users watch a wordless introductory animation explaining the app and practice with a few simple shapes, arranging their physical blocks in front of the iPad with the reflective device installed onto the camera. Musical and visual clues will let users know when they have correctly arranged their blocks. Once they get the hang of it, users may opt for easy, medium, or hard levels before embarking on their shape-filled exploration. A "harder" level is offered, but Tangram enthusiasts must unlock this level by completing puzzles.

TeleStory (iOS): Telestory offers users the chance to write, direct, star in, and film their own TV shows. When the app opens, would-be thespians, directors, and camera operators chose a template upon which to base their stories. The templates include "eye spy," "star adventure," "the band," and "the news." The children then select from a choice of typical scenes for the theme they selected (e.g., in the news theme, children may choose from weather, sports, breaking news, the beat, etc.). Next, users determine which cue card relates to the kind of scene they wish to film. If none of the cards shown work for them, the app allows kids to create their own cue cards. If they aren't laughing yet, they will be when they assume different identities through the use of costumes included in the app. Cartoon costume overlays snap to the face of the star and move as he or she moves. This technology isn't perfect, but users will be having so much fun, they will barely notice. A 3-2-1 countdown initiates the filming. Kids may choose to write, act out, and film as many scenes as they like to complete their TV shows. Shows are saved within the app to My Creations and may be exported to the iPad camera roll for projecting and sharing.

There's No Place Like Space (iOS): Beloved character the Cat in the Hat and his silly set of friends, Thing 1 and Thing 2, join with animated youngsters Dick and Sally in the first Cat in the Hat's Learning Library adventure. Users choose either "read it myself" or "read to me" before they blast off in a rocket on a scientific exploration of the planets. Vocabulary and presentation are geared to be easily understood by the target age range, five to eight. Users touch words or objects to see the words spelled out and hear them spoken. Text boxes with additional facts open with a tap. The text, illustrations, and narration are full of lyrical Seussian charm. There's No Place Like Space strikes the proper balance between fun and learning.

Tickle (iOS): Tickle presents visually based, Scratch-inspired programming for a multitude of devices, including the Star Wars bot BB8, a large selection of drones, the Dash & Dot robotic duo, Arduino Bean, Philips Hue lighting, and the robots Sphero and Ollie. Users select from a large variety of color-coded action and command blocks that lock together like those famous plastic interlocking building blocks, Legos®, to create a seamless code. When the app opens, users choose their device (users might also opt to use cartoon characters and create a project without a device) and are then shown a screen with a simple command project already created for them. Users may choose to edit that project by dragging and dropping in new blocks or delete it entirely and create their own.

Titanic: Her Journey (iOS): The History Press, a publisher dedicated to bringing history to the masses, gathered together the research for Titanic: Her Journey from their fleet of *Titanic* authors and created an app that is both academically complete and brilliantly designed. Users open the app to a series of menus that provide access to a detailed account of the history of *Titanic*, including text, photographs, and other media. The app presents an exhaustive investigation, from her humble shipyard beginnings to the fatal night of her sinking and beyond. The depth and breadth of the information provided is astounding. Users follow not only the ship itself but passengers and crew as well. Included in the sea of fascinating facts are detailed deck plans (and everything you could want to know about the *Titanic*'s construction), biographies of passengers and crew, a cool Did You Know? section with unusual facts users are likely not to have known, and an archive full of interesting photographs, audio, and film. Those familiar with *Titanic*'s tragic tale will find much new information to enthusiastically pore over. Even those only slightly interested in the *Titanic* will find themselves enthralled.

Toca Robot Lab (iOS): There is no learning curve for users of Toca Boca's Robot Lab app. Kids will dive right in, choosing to build their robot from one of three templates: sets of legs, bodies, head, and right and then left arms. The materials offered are all scrap items, sending a subtle message about the benefits of recycling. Once the robot is complete, users fly it through the test lab, a small obstacle course, earning the robot's certification. Each session offers users new sets of recycled materials from which to create a seemingly endless variety of robots. Toca Robot Lab is truly as described, a "digital toy."

Toddler Email Lite (iOS and Android): This app allows precocious tots to receive emails from any of four nursery-rhyme characters (a 99-cent upgrade to the full version offers email from any of 12 nursery-rhyme characters). The emails are perfectly safe, as they come from within the app itself. Users must "log in" by choosing a pictorial answer to the question of "How's the weather?" Once inside their inbox, children are greeted with the familiar "You've got mail." They can see who the mail is from (e.g., Little Bo Peep, the Sheep, the Muffin Man, or the Muffin) and what the subject heading is (e.g., Count My Cupcakes, Bake a Word, Can You Find Me, etc.). Tapping on the subject heading reveals an email presenting an educational opportunity to practice counting, spelling, or memory skills. They may also tap the Get Email button to receive new messages or the Friends button to see a list of their nursery-rhyme friends. (*Note:* In the lite version, users will see grayed-out icons representing the friends they could have if they upgraded to the paid full version.) This educational app is a fun way to allow little ones to imitate their parents and older siblings and feel big and important too. The free lite version of this app is only available for the iPad. Android users must purchase the full version.

Toddler Toy Factory Free (iOS): After opening the app, users will be presented the choice to Make, Find, or Ship. Choosing Make puts little ones in charge of toy creation. A Seussian-like toy machine appears on the screen. Familiar-looking letter blocks also appear on the screen in random order. Users must insert the letter blocks into the toy machine's intake in the correct order to spell the name of a toy. Above the toy machine intake is a grayed-out version of the letter block that must be inserted first to correctly spell the name of one of 10 toys (the paid version offers 70 toys). Once the letters are properly inserted, the machine spits out the toy, which may then be played with. Until users understand that each grayed-out block atop the intake represents the block that is to be inserted, most little ones will need a bit of grown-up help. In Find, youngsters test their memory and concentration skills by choosing either easy or medium levels of difficulty (the hard level is available only with the paid version) and then matching the toys. Ship provides counting practice as children drag toys into a barrel to pack them for shipping. As each toy is dragged into the barrel, users see the number and hear it counted out. The one negative comes as users must choose between easy or medium levels of difficulty (hard is again available with the paid version only) after each counting screen. This app's activities are the perfect mix of learning (spelling, counting, concentration, memory, and hand-eye coordination) and fun.

Tynker (iOS and Android): Tynker is an essential coding app for beginner and intermediate coders of all ages. Those just starting out might wish to begin with Codey's Quest. This game is a simple introduction to the drag-and-drop, colored, interlocking-block system Tynker uses to write code. The system looks very much like Scratch, as its developers took inspiration from Scratch and other programming languages to create Tynker. Once beginners have completed all the sections of Codey's Quest, mastering a new programming skill in each, they may choose to play different games or move on to the Create area of the app. This area allows users to test out their coding skills by creating their own games, musical projects, and apps. Coders may choose to customize prebuilt games (available in five themes: fantasy, adventure, sci-fi, modern, and spooky) loaded into the app or create their own. Users have the option to work offline if needed. Tynker has also recently added connected device support for the robots Sphero® and Ollie®, the Parrot Rolling Spider Drone®, and the Philips Hue® and Lux® personal lighting systems.

Words for Osmo (iOS): Teach letter recognition, spelling, and build vocabulary with the simple word-guessing game using the letter tiles included in the Osmo® kit and the free Words for Osmo app. Users open the app and choose I Spy, Junior Learning Words, or Custom. They can then opt for Versus (against a friend) or Zen (any number of players). As the game begins, a picture appears on the iPad screen along with the direction "guess this word." A colored circle is filled with the letters comprising the word. One of the circles is blank. It is the user's mission to find the correct letter among the letter tiles and place it in front of the iPad (in the range of the Osmo kit's reflective device mounted on the iPad's camera). Any incorrect guess will be shown at the top of the screen. Users are provided with a generous but limited number of incorrect guesses. Registering online for an Osmo account allows users to upload their own photos and create a list of sight words, spelling words, and so on. This child-appropriate take on Hangman will make learning _un!

TECHNOLOGY GLOSSARY

Cubelets: Each of these magnetic cube-shaped building blocks has a specific function that when combined allow users to instantly create a multitude of robots with different abilities. Users need no prior programming experience to enjoy learning with Cubelets. The six-pack starter kit includes six magnetic blocks and a set of robot project cards with instructions. The real fun comes when testing the many other combinations not provided on the project cards and seeing what other types of robots may be made. Though Cubelets are recommended for children aged four and up, they are appropriate for older children as well.

littleBits: Would-be inventors explore the world of circuitry by magnetically snapping together electronically wired pieces or "bits" to create their own unique inventions. Users need no prior knowledge of electrical circuits to begin using littleBits. The starter kit comes with detailed, step-by-step instructions that create a base of knowledge that allows children to build on their new skills and bring their electrical ideas to fruition. The manufacturer recommends littleBits for children aged eight and up.

MaKey MaKey: Connecting a MaKey MaKey board to your laptop with a USB cable in simple plug-and-play fashion and attaching alligator clips to any conductive material (e.g., fruits and vegetables, aluminum foil, coins, Play-Doh®, etc.) allows users to make their computer act as if they are pressing computer keys when, in fact, they are actually touching the conductive material. Straight out of the box, with no prior knowledge of electrical circuits or programming, users can access the MaKey MaKey website to play preprogrammed games and musical instruments by tapping the attached conductive materials. This works because your computer has been fooled by the MaKey MaKey into thinking users are tapping the space bar and arrow keys and clicking the mouse. It is much less complicated than it sounds. The manufacturer recommends the MaKey MaKey for ages eight to infinity, but with supervision the MaKey MaKey is fun for all ages.

Ollie: Ollie is an app-enabled, cylindrical-shaped robot with wheel-like treads. Users download the Ollie app onto their iPads or tablets and command Ollie to move, perform tricks, or change color. Ollie is built for durability and may be used indoors or outdoors. Ollie can now use the Draw 'n' Drive app, originally designed for Ollie's sibling bot, Sphero, where users trace a line on the iPad or tablet and Ollie re-creates the line on whatever surface it is placed upon. Ollie users may also try their hands at Sphero's Macrolab app to create simple programs for Ollie to follow. If desired, Ollie may also be programmed with the free Tickle app. Ollie is recommended for ages eight and up, but with supervision children of all ages will enjoy exploring Ollie's capabilities.

Osmo: The Osmo kit extends the educational capabilities of an iPad by allowing users to take advantage of new ways to learn without tapping, swiping, or typing. The Osmo starter kit includes a white plastic base to hold the iPad upright, allowing hands-free learning; a red reflector to be placed over the iPad's camera so that the iPad can "see" objects placed in front of it; a set of brightly colored wooden tangram blocks; and a complete set of tiles representing the individual letters of the alphabet. Osmo has created a line of free apps designed to encourage self-directed learning through games, play, and exploration in a variety of subjects, including letter recognition, spelling, art, math, and strategic thinking.

Snap Circuits: Learning about electricity and electrical circuits is literally a snap with Snap Circuits. The colorful plastic electronically wired pieces attach together with metal snaps. All Snap Circuits come with easy-to-follow visual guidebooks to help would-be inventors snap together successful electrical projects. Once users build their confidence and knowledge with the included projects, they will want to move on to creating inventions of their own. We recommend splurging on at least one educational kit, which includes student and teacher guides. We purchased the Snap Circuits Extreme® Educational 750 Exp kit, which at the time of publication included the greatest quantity of components and the most extensive student and teacher guides.

Sphero: Sphero is an app-enabled robotic ball that is supported by a collection of apps that allow users to drive, draw, play games, take photos and videos, and create simple programs. Sphero is less durable and might be more difficult to control than its sibling bot, Ollie. In addition to Sphero's Macrolab app, Sphero may also be programmed with the free Tickle app. The manufacturer recommends Sphero for ages eight and up, but with supervision Sphero is fun for all ages. A new, clear, and educational version of Sphero called the Sphero SPRK has recently been released.

WaterColorBot!: The WaterColorBot! is a watercolor-painting robot invented by a 12-year-old girl that translates a digital design into a traditional watercolor painting. Technological artists connect a computer to the WaterColorBot! and use a choice of software to either paint a preloaded design or translate a composition drawn on the computer. No special art supplies are needed. The WaterColorBot! comes with the standard eight-color watercolor paint palette, plastic paintbrush, and a small supply of watercolor paper. Users may inexpensively replenish these items or swap out the paints for markers, pencils, or other drawing implements. The manufacturer provides no recommended age specification for this product.

INDEX

About the Authors

LYNN PAWLOSKI is coauthor of *The Maker Cookbook: Recipes for Children's and 'Tween Library Programs*, has copresented an ALSC webinar on children's programming, has contributed to *Public Libraries* magazine, and has spoken at numerous library and education conferences. She was corecipient with Cindy Wall of the 2015 Faith Hektoen Award for an outstanding program or project that has made a significant impact on library service for children in Connecticut. Pawloski has worked in both school and public libraries. She enjoys developing programs in which children are encouraged to use all avenues of their imagination and finds infinite inspiration in their discoveries.

CINDY WALL is the coauthor of Libraries Unlimited's *The Maker Cookbook: Recipes for Children's and 'Tween Library Programs*. Wall reviews books and apps for *School Library Journal* and has appeared as a guest blogger on its Touch and Go blog. She has copresented an ALSC webinar on children's programming, cowritten an article for *Public Libraries* magazine, and spoken at numerous library and education conferences. Wall won the Connecticut Library Association Publicity Award as well as an LSTA grant to expand her iPad programming, and she was co-recipient with Lynn Pawloski of the 2015 Faith Hektoen Award for an outstanding program or project that has made a significant impact on library service for children in Connecticut.